More Praise for *Unsportsmanlike Conduct*

"Few subjects are as difficult, or as important, as this one, and Jessica Luther handles it flawlessly. We have to demand that schools take better care of our kids; it's that simple. Luther gives us the tools to do so, breaking down exactly where we are, how we got here, and—most importantly—how the system can change." —Rachel Nichols, ESPN

"Jessica Luther is one of the most important voices on gender issues in sports. And this book does not disappoint: it is essential reading for anyone who hopes to better understand the intersection of gender and our sports landscape." —Kate Fagan, espnW

"The maxim of the law is silence gives consent. Back when nobody was talking about AIDS, the maxim was silence equals death. There exists in our major sports a malignant culture of sexual assault and bureaucratic indifference. There is nothing this culture resists more than plain talk, and Jessica Luther has been speaking more plainly about this ongoing obscenity than almost anyone else. This is a hard, necessary, and important book, a book by someone who refuses to be silent, and damn sure refuses to consent." —Charles P. Pierce, author of *Idiot America: How Stupidity Became a Virtue in the Land of the Free*

"Luther's well-researched book speaks powerfully to the complicated landscape of sexual assaults on college campuses—including the greedy interests at play in denying it—and provides us a much-needed road map for instituting effective change. I highly recommend this book for anyone who believes that student safety should matter more than athletic success, and that we all have a role to play in assuring that it does."
—Wendy Davis, former Texas state senator, founder of Deeds Not Words

"*Unsportsmanlike Conduct* is an important book by an important writer. Jessica Luther's place as both sports fan and empathetic observer makes her perfect to explore the shameful ways universities and their athletic programs address sexual assault, as no one could say she doesn't love football. She just loves people more, as she should, and this book is an important mirror to make us question how sports became more important to the world than the women who make life possible."
—Bomani Jones, ESPN

"In painstaking and passionate detail, Jessica Luther challenges those of us who have become seduced by the emotion and ritual of sport to stop being willfully ignorant about the significant problem of sexual assault and sexual violence. Sports, for many of us, have always been characterized as a lighthearted escape from the problems that dominate 'real life,' but this book reminds us that our ability to compartmentalize and rationalize these terrible crimes has cost us our collective humanity."

—Jemele Hill, ESPN

"Luther uses the language and framework of college athletics—a playbook—to demonstrate the industry's systemic problems with sexual violence. This book should be handed to every incoming freshman, and left on the seats of stadiums across the country. A must-read for athletes, coaches, administrators, journalists, and fans alike."

—Katie Nolan, host of Fox Sports' *Garbage Time*

"Jessica Luther has delivered a searing account of the way America's universities and athletic departments have time and again valued winning football games over justice and compassion. *Unsportsmanlike Conduct* is more than an indictment of the culture of big-time college football, it is a call to action to change it."   —Ben Strauss, coauthor of *Indentured: The Inside Story of the Rebellion Against the NCAA*

Janelle Matous

JESSICA LUTHER is an independent writer and investigative journalist living in Austin, Texas. Her work on sports and culture has appeared in the *Texas Observer* and the *Austin Chronicle*, and at *Sports Illustrated*, *Texas Monthly*, *Vice Sports*, *Guardian Sport*, and *Bleacher Report*. Luther's work gained national attention in August 2015 when writing for *Texas Monthly*; she and Dan Solomon broke open the story about a Baylor football player on trial for sexual assault, a case known by only a few in the community and not reported in the media for nearly two years.

UNSPORTSMANLIKE CONDUCT

COLLEGE FOOTBALL AND THE POLITICS OF RAPE

JESSICA LUTHER

EDGE
of SPORTS

Unsportsmanlike Conduct is the third title in Dave Zirin's **Edge of Sports** imprint. Addressing issues across many different sports at both the professional and nonprofessional/collegiate level, Edge of Sports aims to provide an even deeper articulation about the daily collision between sports and politics, giving cutting-edge writers the opportunity to fully explore their areas of expertise in book form.

Published by Akashic Books
©2016 Jessica Luther

ISBN: 978-1-61775-491-3
Library of Congress Control Number: 2016935062

All rights reserved
First printing

Edge of Sports
c/o Akashic Books
Twitter: @AkashicBooks
Facebook: AkashicBooks
E-mail: info@akashicbooks.com
Website: www.akashicbooks.com

This book is dedicated to:

Everyone who has told their story even when they knew they wouldn't be believed.

All who have yet to tell their story.

Each person who has stood alongside those they knew had been harmed and supported them.

Those who have gone up against the system, a system, any system, and demanded acknowledgment, change, and/or justice.

ACKNOWLEDGMENTS

Thank you to:

Dave Zirin, who has believed in my work from the beginning, probably before I ever did.

Johnny Temple and the team at Akashic for taking on this project and doing so with care and compassion.

Dan. It's really something to find a friend who is also a writer, who is smart, who is thoughtful, who lives in your city and likes to work across the table from you in coffee shops, and who is strongest exactly where you are weakest. I owe Dan credit for the framing of this book (the "playbook" concept), something I struggled mightily to articulate on my own and probably wouldn't have been able to do without his help.

Liss, my emotional rock, who is a brilliant writer and thinker, and who makes me better at both through her friendship and her endless kindness.

Laurie, for saving me when I needed to be saved.

Neil, Jim, Carolyn, and Julie, for showing me and teaching me how to be a great researcher.

Tope, Tyler, Katie, Lou, Kavitha, Sydette, Lindsay, Mariame, Lili, David, Shireen, Annie, Soraya, Joel, Julie, Lauren, Andrea, Claire, Travis, Stacey, Claudia, Chloe, Jamil, Caitlin, Diana, and every other person who has conversed with me about the topic and themes in this book, and whose work challenges me to do better all the time. This list is woefully short and undoubtedly I have left off people's names who have influenced and helped shape the work in this book. I am lucky to have so many amazing people in my life.

Every editor who has allowed me to write on this topic and has fought for me and my work before and after publication, especially Emma and Tomas.

Twitter, which has brought people into my life who have radically altered it for the better, who challenge my beliefs and make me see more, and who give me great joy all the time.

All the people who have given their time and love to helping care for my son and have made it possible for me to find the time to do this work.

Every romance author who has written a book that has allowed me to escape, for even one moment, the weight of this work.

My parents (and I am blessed with many) and my sister. For all the love and support throughout my life, I cannot thank you enough. The best cheerleaders, the lot of you.

My son, for your smile, hugs, jokes, and adventures.

Finally, nothing on these pages would ever exist without the support from my partner in life, Aaron. He is the best of them and I am grateful every day that I get to laugh alongside and with him. Circle and thumbs-up.

Despite all of this help, I want to be clear: the work in this book is my own, and while these people all deserve credit for what makes it good, I take full responsibility for whatever is not.

TABLE OF CONTENTS

Editor's Foreword 15

Introduction: The Playbook 21

PART I: THE PLAYBOOK AS IT IS

Chapter 1: The Field 39

Chapter 2: What the Playbook Doesn't Show 61

Chapter 3: Nothing to See Here 83

Chapter 4: The Shrug 106

Chapter 5: Moving On 130

PART II: HOW IT COULD BE

Play #1: Consent Is Cool; Get Some 155

Play #2: Understand Trauma 164

Play #3: Go Federal 174

Play #4: Intervene, Maybe 175

Play #5: Follow the Players 184

Play #6: Be Specific 187

Play #7: Teach Coaches to Teach Boys to Be Men 189

Play #8: Clean It Up 196

Play #9: Fire People 198

Play #10: Do Anything 200

Play #11: Do Better 204

Play #12: Calm Down 211

Play #13: Hire Women 214

Conclusion: Change Is Possible 218

Endnotes 225

Editor's Foreword

Rape is one of the most terrible crimes on earth and it happens
every few minutes. The problem with groups who deal with rape
is that they try to educate women about how to defend themselves.
What really needs to be done is teaching men not to rape.

—Kurt Cobain

The world of sports has a sexual assault problem the same
way one can say that Miami has a global warming problem.
In other words, it's true, but it's also an issue that extends well
beyond just this one corner of the planet. The sports world is
not a hermetically sealed arena, cut off from the real world; it
is here in this real world where we need to begin the discussion
about understanding humanity's entrenched culture of gender
violence.

The world has a violence-against-women and sexual assault problem. According to the World Health Organization,
35 percent of all women globally are survivors of some form
of violence. Then there is the United States. This country has
a violence-against-women and sexual assault problem, with
numbers just below the global average; the Justice Department
estimates that 68 percent of rapes are not reported to law enforcement. Our college campuses have a sexual assault problem.
These institutions of higher learning are places where one in five

women say that they have faced sexual violence, with 80 percent of all cases not reported. We also know that the issue is handled terribly by too many universities. According to the Department of Education's Office for Civil Rights, at least 183 colleges and universities are currently under federal investigation for mishandling sexual assault claims on their campuses.

We know as well that on many campuses, sports are at the heart of campus life and athletes are deified, entitled campus leaders who have a tremendous amount of influence on their communites. These heroes are more likely to commit and be charged with sexual assault. One study showed that college athletes make up 3.3 percent of male students but 19 percent of those accused of sexual assault. A 2012 Rutgers analysis found something similar and the *Boston Globe* put it, "It is unclear whether college athletes are more likely to commit sexual crimes than other students. But we see a unique sense of entitlement, sexual and otherwise, among some male college athletes, especially those in high-profile or revenue-producing sports."

Or, as Jessica Luther wrote on social media, in a post that inspired us to approach her to write this trailblazing book, "The stories about campus administrations or athletic depts. failing to do a damn thing about sexual violence are endless . . . Yesterday I just told someone I couldn't pursue one because I was already working on three other ones. I have that same conversation at least twice a week at this point."

The point here is simple: we have a problem that without question exists independently of sports, yet we also have a lot of data that says it's worse in sports. In recent years colleges like Missouri, Vanderbilt, Florida State, and Tennessee have seen such cases. These stories are chained together by the blaringly obvious yet little-discussed relationship between male jock culture and rape culture. Everyone who either cares about stopping the violence or about the lessons produced by sports has an obligation to educate themselves on the issue and speak out.

It is for all of these reasons that *Unsportsmanlike Conduct* was a book that needed to be written. Jock culture has morphed into rape culture on too many campuses, and we in the sports media have been silent about it for far too long. Right now, many of the institutions of higher learning discussed in these pages are attempting to grapple with this reality. Yet it often feels like so much flailing: trying to cover gaping wounds with bandages or shoveling sand into the ocean just to be able to say, *Hey, we're trying!*

These cases tend to be viewed in isolation from one another: individual instances on different campuses. They are rarely examined systemically—as a symptom of a college sports landscape that exploits so-called student-athletes and then far too often excuses any and all behavior as a method of payment. Now that people are finally talking about this issue, we desperately need to expand this discussion, and *Unsportsmanlike Conduct* fills the gap. This was a book that needed to be written but could not have been written by anyone other than Jessica Luther, who we knew we could trust to tell this story the way it needed to be told. With a track record going back years, Luther has covered this story with a relentless consistency that no one on the sportswriting landscape can match. She also provides a framework that ensures the reader will not throw up her or his hands with despair or seek out easy scapegoats. This is in fact more than a book; it is a tool to help crack the code of why these assaults keep happening. This will help athletic departments—if they are willing to listen—to cease being examples of what is wrong with university life and help make them the leaders they need to be in the push to stop the violence.

—Dave Zirin, Editor, Edge of Sports Books

This is a book about college football and sexual violence. There's nothing easy about what lies ahead in the following pages. I will not sanitize descriptions of violence, and violence is what this book is about. It's a kind of violence that is all around us all the time, that affects so many people, often repeatedly throughout their lives. This is a warning then for those who might be triggered by descriptions of sexual violence or interpersonal violence. If you turn back now, get to a point in the book and put it down to never return, skim over large chunks, or read it in short, manageable pieces, then you will, in some way, mirror my own process of writing this. Dealing so directly with this kind of everyday violence that we are constantly forced to make sense of is hard emotional work. Reading this will be that too.

It's worth it, though. Because we need to have this conversation and we need to be honest when we do it.

INTRODUCTION
The Playbook

I.

I was born with garnet and gold blood. Both of my parents graduated from Florida State University (FSU). Growing up, I spent Saturday afternoons in the autumn watching FSU football, either sitting next to my dad in front of a TV or in the stands of Doak Campbell Stadium. When it came time for me to go to college, I only applied to one school. And during the four years I was at Florida State, I went to every home game, sweating in the blistering heat of an early-season eleven a.m. start or freezing cold during mid-November rivalry games against Florida.

I learned early on how to be a fan. There are rules and rituals the fans of a sports team follow and do, a kind of collective performance before and during games that show the love for our school and team. The playbook for fans consists of memorizing chants, wearing the right colors, painting our faces, and always singing along whenever you hear the school's fight song. The most important play, though, is the one where you give your team your love and devotion, and you trust in the players and coaches even when they play badly and even if you have to ignore what they do when they are off the field and out of uniform. This, the fan playbook prescribes, is what good fans do.

I used to be a really good FSU fan.

On January 4, 2000, in the middle of my sophomore year, I was sitting high in the stands of the Superdome in New Orleans, watching Chris Weinke and Peter Warrick lead FSU to a national championship (they defeated Michael Vick's Virginia Tech Hokies 46–29). I stayed for the trophy presentation, crawling along the seats until I was positioned in front of the stage where Warrick accepted the Most Valuable Player award. I collected newspapers the next day that had headlines about our championship win, and when I got back to Florida, I painstakingly cut out pictures and articles, combined them with photographs I had taken, and made myself a scrapbook so I would always remember how great that experience was. I'm sure somewhere in my attic is a T-shirt from that year with the words *Wire-to-Wire* on it (FSU was the only team to start the year No. 1 and keep the ranking all the way through).

I remember, before and during the championship game, justifying to myself and any Virginia Tech fan who would listen that Warrick deserved to be on the field despite having been arrested late in September 1999 for grand theft. In collusion with a store clerk at a Tallahassee Dillard's, he and FSU wide receiver Laveranues Coles stole hundreds of dollars' worth of merchandise. After they both pleaded down to misdemeanor petty theft, Coles was kicked off the team (he was already on probation for an earlier incident). Warrick, easily the most famous person on the team, an integral part of the offense, and without a prior record, was only suspended two games. I had no problem with any of this, mainly because I paid almost no attention to it. I kept my eyes on the prize of a football championship and my trust in FSU's coach, Bobby Bowden. But I was also 100 percent sure it was fair that Warrick was playing.[1]

Over the past decade or so, I've suffered through the years of mediocre FSU football, always believing my team could do it, then watching sadly as they collapsed once again. Don't bring up the name Chris Rix around me. I am still sad over the way Xavier Lee's potential never matched up with his play. And I remember the name Drew Weatherford because I am apparently a masochist who likes to continually cause myself pain by reliving the later 2000s.

But then the 2013 season happened. FSU once again had a defense. And an O-line. And, most famously, we had Jameis Winston at quarterback.

Winston was the No. 1 quarterback recruit in 2012. He redshirted during the 2012–13 season and came out of the gates blazing in 2013. In the sixth week of the season, No. 5 FSU marched into No. 3 Clemson's stadium and put up more points than any other opponent ever had in Death Valley. Winston had 444 passing yards, three touchdowns, and a lot of serious Heisman chatter.

He was a damn good football player. And I was still a damn good fan, telling anyone who would listen about my team's brand-new quarterback who was going to take us places.

Then, suddenly, my fandom crashed headlong into my work, which often interrogates the intersection of sport and interpersonal violence. Only a few days apart in November 2013, the *Tampa Bay Times* and *TMZ* both made public-records requests to the Tallahassee police department (TPD).[2] It turns out that what they were looking for would usher in one of the highest-profile college football sexual assault cases in years: a female student had reported to the TPD in December 2012 that Jameis Winston had raped her.

My fan playbook failed me. I wanted so desperately to have some way to make sense of the team I loved being piloted by a potentially violent player, one apparently shielded from consequence by his team, the university—*my* university—and the local police. I needed a new playbook. So, I decided to write one.

II.

This is not a book about Jameis Winston. This is not even a book about football players. This is a book about the intersection of college football and sexual assault, and the people and systems that ignore, minimize, and even perpetuate this violence; the Winston case just happens to be a thorough and high-profile example of what that intersection looks like. And it happens to involve the school and team I've loved my whole life.

In the late summer and early fall of 2013, I was watching two college football sexual assault cases play out, one at Navy and another Vanderbilt. Four Vanderbilt football players had been arrested and charged that August with raping a fellow student. As that was playing out in Nashville, there was a trial up the road in Annapolis of three Navy football players who had been charged with abusive sexual conduct or aggravated sexual assault. The majority of media interested in the cases were local newspapers and TV stations, while national sports media were more focused on whether a famous college quarterback, Johnny Manziel, had gotten paid for his signature and if he would get punished for it. (That story died quickly and he never was censured.)

Then, in mid-September, I began working on a piece for the *Atlantic* about college football recruiting practices and how they used women. In that piece I argued that treating women like prizes creates an atmosphere wherein women's consent takes a backseat to what football players feel they are owed. I brought up the Navy and Vanderbilt cases, and mentioned a couple of other ones I had found.

I became interested in trying to understand both the reasons these cases did not make the news and also if they were part of larger historical patterns. I started to find mentions of, links to, and footnotes about previous football players accused, and some found guilty, of rape, dating back to the 1970s. To keep track of it all, I started a list online of every allegation or case I found, a list which continues to grow to this day. To keep tabs on it all, I created Google alerts relating to sports and interpersonal violence, including "football rape." And I have been keeping tabs ever since.

III.

Football teams create playbooks, in which they draw up the plays they will use on the field. A page in the book looks like the measured lines on a green football field, offensive and defensive players sketched onto it using symbols like circles and triangles or Xs and Os. The movement of the players, the routes they are to run on the field, are represented by lines tipped with arrows pointing the direction they should move if everything in the play goes as planned. Coaches and players memorize these playbooks. Each individual play is given a name, the intricate detailed performance boiled down to a word or phrase. The plays can be communicated in a matter of seconds from coach to player, sideline to field, quarterback to the offensive line, on and on. It is the complicated made simple. If all goes well, the large amount of work that goes into a single play suddenly looks like a natural flow of bodies moving in unison that result in the movement of the ball down the field or the successful stop of the other team's offense, a seemingly obvious outcome despite it all happening in an unscripted and chaotic setting where so many things could have taken place instead.

Playbooks are why teams work, how they move information quickly, and how they become successful on the field.

This book is about a different kind of playbook—the one coaches, teams, universities, police, communities, the media, and fans seem to follow whenever a college football player is accused, charged, and/or convicted of sexual assault. When these cases break, it often feels like everyone involved is following the same script, making the choices that mirror other cases, doing the exact thing we've come to expect based on whatever has transpired before. It is as if our society has its own collective Xs, Os, and lines tipped with arrows drawn on pages we all have access to, read through, and have memorized. The plays are popular narratives we all know about athletes or women who report sexual violence against them, and they are the familiar responses of the people in charge, the seemingly natural patterns and progressions that these cases take. Everyone plays their part, they run their routes, and the nuance and detail of complicated cases is suddenly flattened in a way that makes how we react to it all seem normal or natural; each case is so easily boiled down in a society that often minimizes the complicated reality of sexual violence.

This book unpacks the societal playbook piece by piece, drawing attention to each X and O, and explores the possibility of destroying the old plays and replacing them with ones that will force us to finally do something about this issue.

IV.

There are plenty of reasons we often talk about sexual assault when it involves a sports star: players are high profile, and because of the money invested in them or their teams, people can feel a certain ownership over them; players are held in high esteem by fans or hated by fans of rival teams, and so their off-the-field behavior is either a shock or evidence of what we already knew; players in legal trouble are often not able to play, so that could have an effect on the team; many athletes are African American, especially in football, and because of the racism that exists independently and around the world of sports, the US media as well as the legal system often focus on crime when the perpetrators are black. At the collegiate level, there is a personal investment in the fandom from people who attended that school, who pour money into the institution, and who might see the players on their team representing the university and so also themselves in some part.

On top of all of this, football is the most popular sport in the US. It makes a lot of money for a lot of people. College football is now second to the NFL in overall sports revenues. Universities are often financially invested in major sports, so officials—and highly paid coaches, making literally a hundred times what they earned forty years ago—have some motivation to absolve players and move on as if nothing happened. The issue is so deeply rooted that Senator Claire McCaskill's report on sexual assaults on college campuses, released in July 2014, found that "approximately 20 percent of the nation's largest public institutions and 15 percent of the largest private institutions allow their athletic departments to oversee cases involving student athletes."[3]

This is not completely surprising. The power of football can stretch all the way into the courtroom too. In 2004, six Brigham Young football players (former and current) were charged in connection to the rape of a seventeen-year-old girl. Two went to trial and one of the other players testified against them, saying on the stand, "We knew we had done something that was wrong. We took advantage of a girl that we shouldn't have." After the jury acquitted the players, the prosecutor says, one of the jury members told her the players had suffered enough because "they lost their scholarships" and "they were kicked off the team."[4]

V.

All of this together is paradoxical: there are cultural power structures that surround football players and protect them from having to answer for the violence they commit; but the very importance of the sport and our fascination with it means that we pay more attention to these power structures than the ones that operate in everyday cases where the perpetrator is not a public figure. In untangling how players are protected and why, we can use this microcosm to see larger societal forces at play that protect all kinds of people, guilty or innocent, who are accused of sexual or interpersonal violence.

The problem of sexual violence is a cultural one, not limited to any single group. In 2011, the Centers for Disease Control and Prevention determined that "an estimated 19.3 percent of women and 1.7 percent of men [in the United States] have been raped during their lifetimes," with "an estimated 43.9 percent of women and 23.4 percent of men [who said they] experienced other forms of sexual violence during their lifetimes."[5] According to the Rape, Abuse & Incest National Network (often referred to as RAINN), 17.6 percent of all women will be raped or victims of attempted rape in their lifetime.[6] Almost the exact same percentage, 17.7 percent, is true for all white women, while black women have a slightly higher chance at 18.8 percent while only making up 13.2 percent of the population, and Native American women are staggeringly high at 34.1 percent despite being only 1.2 percent of the population. In December 2014, Callie Marie Rennison, a criminology professor at the University of Colorado at Denver, published a piece in the *New York Times* where she wrote that she and her colleague, Lynn A. Addington at American University, "found that the estimated rate of sexual assault and rape of female college students, ages eighteen to twenty-four, was 6.1 per 1,000 students. This is nothing to be proud of, but it is significantly lower than the rate experienced by women that age who don't attend college—8 per 1,000."[7] In short, economically disadvantaged women, who are "in the lowest income bracket, with annual household incomes of less than $7,500, are sexually victimized at 3.7 times the rate of women with household incomes of $35,000 to $49,999, and at about six times the rate of women in the highest income bracket (households earning $75,000 or more annually)." On top of this, economics break along racial lines. According to a report by the Pew Research Center in December 2014, published at the same time as Rennison's piece, "The wealth of white households was thirteen times the median wealth of black households in 2013, compared with eight times the wealth in 2010" and "the wealth of white households is now more than ten times the wealth of Hispanic households, compared with nine times the wealth in 2010."[8] All of this, taken together, suggests that the people most likely to be victims of sexual assault in the US are economically disadvantaged women of color.

And yet, we are currently having a cultural moment regarding college campus sexual assault. In a country of roughly 319 million people, about 6.5 percent (twenty-one million) attend college, according to the National Center for Education Statistics.[9] And that 6.5 percent is made of a particular slice of the population. As Rebecca Klein wrote in the *Huffington Post* in October 2014, "Students who went to low-minority, higher-income suburban schools were the most likely to have enrolled in college. Among higher-income schools, those with high populations of minority students posted lower college enrollment rates than low-minority schools."[10] This is interesting when you consider the statistics above about victims of sexual assault. Certainly our focus on college sexual assault stems in part from our cultural tendency to pay far more attention to the experiences of white, middle/upper-class Americans. We have idealized dreams about what college is supposed to represent in the lives of young adults, a time of exploration, surrounded by peers and learning, all in preparation for going out into the world and becoming somebody. There is no space in these wishful aspirations for the realities of sexual violence that we find everywhere else. Another aspect of the focus on college sexual assault is that tackling it seems doable; after all, we are only talking about a small percentage of the population in a confined space.

All of this combined is why we have seen an ever-increasing series of laws over the last few decades that are supposed to help mitigate, even eradicate sexual violence in this one particular part of our culture. Under Title IX (the federal statute best known for requiring gender parity in sports), which became law in 1972, a university receiving federal assistance must ensure that every person who attends the school has equal access to educational opportunities. A campus with known sexual predators within the student body is an obstacle to that access; universities that do not adequately protect students from sexual assault or ignore reported assaults are, therefore, in danger of losing federal funding. It's worth noting that as of early 2016, no university has ever lost federal funding for Title IX violations.

The most difficult aspect of Title IX has always been enforcement. Since the crime of sexual assault is rarely reported, how do we measure if universities are doing enough? Victims of sexual assault are often afraid or ashamed to report the attack, or they fear they'll be blamed for the circumstances of the assault. When they do speak up, they are often not believed. As one consequence, only a fraction of rapists land behind bars.

Nevertheless, the 1990 Clery Act (a.k.a. the Crime Awareness and Campus Security Act) created standardized reporting requirements, necessitating colleges to be more transparent about crimes taking place on their campuses; the law has been amended and broadened several times.

The latest amendment, enacted in 2013, is called the Campus Sexual Violence Elimination Act, or Campus SaVE Act. In order to comply with Title IX, the Clery Act, and SaVE, universities must perform a list of actions that include collecting data on interpersonal violence, providing victims with information about their right to report, conducting prompt and fair investigations of reported assaults, and educating students on such subjects as how to intervene as bystanders and how to reduce their risk of being assaulted.

President Obama's administration, led principally by Vice President Joe Biden, has worked on the issue from multiple angles, including convening the White House Task Force to Protect Students From Sexual Assault; creating the site NotAlone.gov that provides "information for students, schools, and anyone interested in finding resources on how to respond to and prevent sexual assault on college and university campuses and in our schools"; and starting "It's On Us," a media campaign featuring high-profile actors and athletes who ask people to take a pledge "to recognize that nonconsensual sex is sexual assault, to identify situations in which sexual assault may occur, to intervene in situations where consent has not or cannot be given, and to create an environment in which sexual assault is unacceptable and survivors are supported."

There are also new activist groups who are simultaneously drawing attention to this issue. Know Your IX (referencing Title IX) is "a national survivor-run, student-driven campaign to end campus sexual violence" that educates students on their

rights under the law. End Rape on Campus (EROC) "provides free direct assistance to survivors of all genders who seek
to file federal Office for Civil Rights (Title IX, Title II) and/
or Clery complaints in order to hold colleges and universities
accountable for their handling of sexual violence, and provides
mentorship in campus organizing, survivor support, and policy
reform." EROC was heavily featured in the 2015 documentary
The Hunting Ground for helping dozens of people across the
country file Title IX complaints with the Office of Civil Rights.
Their efforts, along with Know Your IX and other groups like
Students Active for Ending Rape (SAFER) and SurvJustice,
have resulted in more than 180 colleges to date being investigated for not doing their jobs to protect every student's right to
access education, a civil right in the United States.

The combined popularity of the sport of football, the ongoing national discussion around college sexual assault, and the
timing of not only the Jameis Winston case but several other
high-profile cases make this the opportune moment to be discussing the intersection of college football and sexual violence.

VI.

Throughout this book, I will be using a few different terms
that need to be defined before moving on.

"Sexual assault" and **"sexual violence"** are very broad
terms. The Chicago Taskforce on Violence Against Girls &
Young Women's "Reporting on Rape and Sexual Violence" media toolkit says, "'Sexual activity,' 'sexual assault,' and 'molest'
are vague terms that tell us nothing about the actual crime, making it impossible for the public to understand what happened,
or to know how to feel about the harm done and whether the
reactions of responsible adults, law enforcement officials, etc.,
have been appropriate."[11] Because of this vagueness, I will only

use these terms when I am speaking very generally about these crimes, often collectively or as a cultural phenomenon. Otherwise, I will use the most specific language I can to describe the actual violence so there is no confusion about the events I'm discussing.

"Rape" is a much more specific term that refers to someone penetrating another person's body without their consent. The FBI describes it this way: "Penetration, no matter how slight, of the vagina or anus with any body part or object, or oral penetration by a sex organ of another person, without the consent of the victim."[12] While this seems like a settled idea, the FBI only recently updated this definition in January 2012 (becoming effective a year later), after it was determined that the eighty-year-old definition ("The carnal knowledge of a female forcibly and against her will") was too vague. I will use "rape" when talking about cases where one person rapes another person and, if possible and trying not to be gratuitous or sensational, will be specific about how the person raped the other.

"Rape culture" is all around us all the time. It is a culture where people, mainly women, come to expect a form of sexual harassment, assault, or rape at some point, perhaps daily, because we minimize, ignore, or make excuses for the reality of sexual violence in many people's lives. It blames the victim when violence does happen and it rarely punishes the perpetrator for inflicting it. It is a culture where, no matter what the statistics tell us about the rarity of people lying about being sexually assaulted but also the prevalence of sexual violence, it is nonetheless easy to believe the victim is lying.

"Consent" is someone granting someone else the right to touch, hug, caress, kiss, or have sex with them. It can be communicated in a number of ways but it must be communicated in some way. If anyone is not 100 percent sure they have someone's consent, then they don't have it, and should communicate with that person to gain consent before proceeding. It is also the legal concept at the center of sexual assault cases. Minors cannot legally consent to sexual acts, nor can people who are incapacitated (including if someone has had a lot of alcohol to drink, taken drugs, etc.).

VII.

There is much to say about college football and sexual violence, about how it is and how it could be. And so this book is divided into two sections.

First, I sketch out the playbook everyone has been following for decades when someone reports that a college football player has sexually assaulted them. I look at the patterns across the cases I've uncovered and establish the field of play on which this playbook is enacted. After tackling the complicated ways that race, gender, and money affect how we view these cases and the players involved in them, each chapter examines the kinds of plays different groups opt to run in response to reports of sexual violence: universities and their athletic departments ignore them, the National Collegiate Athletic Association (NCAA) keeps its head in the sand, the media try to move on quickly, and fans get mad.

By shining a light directly on this playbook, this book attempts to start multiple conversations around a topic that shows no signs of going away anytime soon.

Second, I draft a new playbook, one full of possibilities for mitigating these problems. It is a desperate list of alternative plays that will be more difficult to implement than what we are used to. But they will push on our established ideas about how the game is played and, in turn, offer the possibility of a better, safer, more fair game in the future.

There is an idea that sports teach kids discipline, rule-following, and sportsmanship. The last is a loosely defined concept that encompasses such things as respect for the opposing team, graciousness in defeat, and humility in victory. True sportsmen are never mean in their interactions with the other team, they are not flagrant in their fouls, and they do not bring violence into the game that goes above and beyond what is written into the games' rule book. In college football, unsportsmanlike conduct can get you thrown off the field. Racial slurs and swinging punches can get you ejected. Because to be unsportsmanlike in your conduct is to destroy the very heart of sport, to make a space governed by rules suddenly dangerously unpredictable and even violent.

In the playbook as it stands now, sexual assault is not an immediate ejection from the game, sometimes not even a foul. It is easy to say that you do not condone this kind of violence; it is infinitely harder to take a hard look at how the very sport you love contributes to a culture that ignores, minimizes, and sometimes perpetrates it. It can feel that to change it is impossible. Let's do that hard look and then let's draw up a new playbook that says sexual assault is, in fact, unsportsmanlike conduct.

To do any of this without first addressing the idea that these cases are isolated events, not part of a larger pattern, would be irresponsible, because there is a pattern if you are willing to see it.

PART I

THE PLAYBOOK AS IT IS

The Field

A playbook only exists if you have a field on which to run your plays. That "field," for this playbook, is a football culture saturated with a masculinity which can manifest in horrible ways.

Football is one of the premier lenses through which we define masculinity in our culture. Who is more masculine than men who take to the football field and run headlong into each other, battering their bodies together, doing what most of us would be terrified to do if placed in that space? But that masculinity can encourage terrible behavior.

In a piece for the *Advocate* in March 2015, Wade Davis, a former NFL prospect and the executive director of You Can Play, an organization whose mission is to help end homophobia in sports, defined masculinity as "the ways in which we expect 'men' to act," but noted that there is no one standard definition.[13] There are a multitude of ways that one can be "masculine," based on the person or grouping defining it. One of the most important ways it is defined is as the absence of the feminine. Davis writes, "If masculinity is idolized, then 'femininity' (another indefinable word) is, by default, demonized, and for many, never as worthy. Sexism, the root of homophobia, creates the conditions for individuals to feel as if they have to perform certain rigid tropes of masculinity and femininity in order to be perceived as normal and acceptable."

In sports, football in particular, masculinity that is considered "normal and acceptable" can be dangerous, both to the players themselves who put their bodies on the line and the people around them in their off-field lives who have to interact with these hypermasculine men. A 1999 study found that the message boys receive when watching sports is that

> *a real man is strong, tough, aggressive, and, above all, a winner in what is still a man's world. To be a winner, he must be willing to compromise his own long-term health by showing guts in the face of danger, by fighting other men when necessary, and by "playing hurt" when he's injured. He must avoid being soft; he must be the aggressor, both on the "battle fields" of sports and in his consumption choices. Whether he is playing sports or making choices about which products to purchase, his aggressiveness will win him the ultimate prize: the adoring attention of beautiful women and the admiration of other men.*[14]

The outcome of this in real life can be confusing. While players are celebrated and financially rewarded for being aggressive, strong fighters on the field, they are demonized for what that masculinity looks like in the rest of their life. As Andre Perry wrote in 2014, to be a man and participate in football culture is to "be a bounty hunter, a missile, a shamer, homophobe, punisher, beater, and extortionist who will get on his knees and be thankful for winning a game."[15]

A large reason we had such a robust discussion around out gay NFL recruit Michael Sam is that homophobia is predicated on the sexist idea that being weak is to be female, or to be female in any way is to be weak. Football players are the height of masculinity, and since we have determined gay men to be feminine, how can you have a football player who is also gay? The answer is that you have to push on antiquated ideas about masculinity. And there's no better space to do that in than football.

In March 2015, the same month Davis published his piece in the *Advocate*, I interviewed him. We were sitting in a large suite in Austin, Texas, the room's wide windows looking out over the river and toward downtown. Reclining casually, one leg propped up so his foot was resting on his knee, Davis talked with me about masculinity and homophobia in football. He told me that gay players and the work that You Can Play is doing are "redefining how people view manhood and masculinity and femininity." Referring to Michael Sam kissing his then-boyfriend on camera on ESPN when he was drafted into the NFL in 2014, Davis said, "What I really love about what Michael did, very few people from the age of probably twelve to seventy will ever be able to say they didn't watch two men be intimate while watching football. And football is the holder of masculinity. To have two men be intimate in that space in a such a public way, you watch Masculinity cry, 'No! Not me! NOT ME! No! No!'"

That matters because of the impact that football culture has on how we think about masculinity. And as Davis explained, football has the power to affect or change the bad parts of modern masculinity.

Still, right now, the masculinity fostered in football locker rooms is often homophobic and incredibly misogynistic. And sometimes it is downright dangerous.

And so, when we look at all the known cases of college football and sexual assault, there are certain patterns that emerge: the prevalence of gang rape, threats against the person who reported, and ease with which people avoid taking responsibility for any of it.

II.

I have collected a list of more than 115 cases of college football sexual assault allegations, spanning from 1974 to 2016. Over the last four decades, through each one of these, coaches, athletic directors, universities, the NCAA, police who investigate the crimes, the media who cover it, and the public who they all report to have learned how to think and talk about the athletes involved, the women who report the crime(s), and every institution that's implicated when there's a failure in the system.

One hundred and ten is not such a high number considering how many college football programs there are and how many men play on each team. But the numbers are not hard and fast. First, many of these cases involve multiple players. Also, the idea that you could be raped by someone other than a stranger is a fairly new concept in and of itself. The term "acquaintance rape" first appeared in print in the late 1970s and didn't go mainstream for another decade. A ripple effect of this is that sexual assault is woefully underreported, especially on college campuses. Finally, it's much easier for me to locate cases from the last decade or so, since newspapers and TV stations began putting their content online. My Google alerts over the last three years have flagged cases that probably would have gone completely under my radar in the past. The list then is top-heavy over the last few years.

Here's a sense of the problem, though. In 2015, there were allegations against players at Florida International University, the University of Tennessee, UCLA, and Santa Barbara City College. 2014 saw cases at Utah State, Kentucky, Tennessee, Oklahoma,

Texas, Tulane, Bowling Green, Tulsa, Culver-Stockon College, Miami, Vanderbilt, Kansas, New Mexico, Ole Miss, and Eastern Washington University. In 2013, there were cases reported at Baylor, Brown, Hobart and William Smith Colleges, Pacific University, Ohio State, Arizona State, Vanderbilt University, McGill University, Wisconsin, and the University of California, Los Angeles. In 2012, there were allegations against players at the University of Texas, Appalachian State University, Baylor, Old Dominion, Morehouse, and the US Naval Academy.

You get the idea.

III.

Many of the sexual assault cases I've found involve multiple athletes as either participants in or witnesses to the sexual violence, which is a particular facet of hypermasculine spaces. In *Fraternity Gang Rape: Sex, Brotherhood, and Privilege on Campus*, Peggy Reeves Sanday says that this behavior is common when there is "a group of persons associated by or as if by ties of brotherhood."[16] These men end up "bonding through sex." Participating in a gang rape "operates to glue the male group as a unified entity," Sanday argues. "It establishes fraternal bonding and helps boys to make the transition to their vision of a powerful manhood—in unity against women, one against the world."

That multiple football players would participate in sexual violence together, a communal act that Sanday says is based around asserting one's masculinity, makes sense considering how important masculinity is to football (and football to masculinity).

There are so many cases of gang rapes involving college football players. It is a depressing and terrifying phenomenon. The earliest case I can locate at all is from Notre Dame in 1974;

it happens to be an allegation of gang rape. The *New York Times* reported it this way in 1976:

> *An 18-year-old South Bend high school student alleged that she had been raped by six black football players, that as many as 20 of the Fighting Irish were aware of the incident and that some even looked on. The unsigned complaint was made by the blonde senior at Sound Bend (Ind.) Memorial Hospital. She had driven there following the alleged rape—at a Notre Dame dormitory—to be examined for injuries. Although unharmed physically, the girl was later temporarily placed under psychiatric care.*[17]

A university administrator called the woman "a queen of the slums with a mattress tied to her back." The charges were dropped quickly, "the girl and her parents [having] requested that no charges be filed against the players—one of whom was her boyfriend." The players were suspended for a year, though, for violating school rules. The *New York Times* piece from 1976 was about their return to the team and the coach who helped them through it all. It's a piece that celebrates the coach for supporting these players through a difficult time, one created, the paper says, by the "so-called victim [who] was described as a football groupie."

But in 2012, Melinda Henneberger, in a piece at the *National Catholic Reporter* (and about a case at Notre Dame from 2010), revealed that a woman had contacted her to say that in 1976, "two of the same young men accused in the [1974 case], along with a third man, were caught in the act of raping her in her dorm room."[18] That woman was told by "a top St. Mary's official" that "one of the men had raped another St. Mary's student as well. And then? 'I was told to shut up and mind my own business,' and she did, until now."

These two earliest cases could almost be described as generic ones. They are part of a pattern that has repeated for decades.

The list of these cases is truly devastating in its length. It is worth taking in how often this happens.

IV.

In 1980, a running back at Oregon, along with three former teammates, was indicted on charges of first-degree sodomy and coercion from a case dating back to 1978, and the Eugene police were looking into possible charges for other players, as they "had talked to a number of women who said they were rape victims."[19]

In 1979, seven players at Kentucky were suspended after they were charged with raping another student. Two years after that, another two players were indicted on sexual assault charges.[20]

In 1986, after a woman reported that four Berkeley players had raped her, the school decided that adequate punishment was for the players to apologize to the woman, go to counseling, and do community service work.[21] The players were never charged. The same year, four players at Clemson were accused of sexually assaulting, kidnapping, and robbing the mother of another player. A grand jury refused to indict. One of the players went on to play in the NFL.

In 1989, two Oklahoma players were convicted of raping a fellow student in a dormitory on campus. In 1992, Nigel Clay, one of those players, told the *Los Angeles Times*, "I don't know how to say it, but, bottom line, I just felt that sometimes, walking around . . . well, speaking for myself and a lot of other people, we felt like we were above the law . . . like OU would protect us from anything."[22]

The list of cases with multiple football players accused goes on.

Miami and Tennessee in 1990. In 1992, two Arkansas players were acquitted of raping a thirteen-year-old girl. East Tennessee and Virginia Tech in 1994.[23]

In 1995, five current and former Idaho State football players were charged with statutory rape for having sex with fourteen- and fifteen-year-old girls.[24] Charges were reduced to misdemeanor battery when the victims refused to testify. At least four of them pleaded guilty and the two then-current players were kicked off the team.

Grambling State in 1996 and Appalachian State the following year. Colorado in 1997 and 2001, and Oregon State in 1998.[25]

In 2000, a woman told her parents that four Oklahoma State players had raped her at a party five months prior in November 1999. "Criminal charges were never filed," the *New York Times* reported she said, "because in the hours following the incident, she had signed a waiver of prosecution after being told by the police that her story had not been corroborated and she did not have a case."[26] She later sued in civil court and settled with two of the players, one of them then a player in the NFL.

In 2000, a then-fifteen-year-old girl at the University of Alabama at Birmingham "was being passed around like a mix tape. In all, she alleges, more than two dozen Blazer athletes [mainly football and basketball players] took their turn."[27]

That is twenty-three cases so far across twenty-five-plus years.

Three football players were kicked out of the Naval Academy in 2001 after a woman reported that they had raped her. In 2002, two players at Iowa State were charged with second-degree sexual abuse. That same year, a woman told police that four Notre Dame players raped her. One man pleaded guilty to sexual battery, one was acquitted, and the charges against the other two were dropped. That same year, a woman at Georgia reported that several members of the football and basketball teams gang raped her.[28]

Then it was Brigham Young University in 2004 and University of Tennessee at Chattanooga in 2005. Two players pleaded guilty to raping a woman in 2006 at SUNY Albany. Two Iowa players were eventually punished for charges stemming from a rape of a woman in 2007. That same year, four Minnesota players were arrested for rape.[29]

In 2010, multiple players at both Missouri and Montana were accused of rape. In 2011, a woman reported that two Appalachian State football players had raped her, and two players and another student had sexually assaulted her. Another woman also reported two of those players for raping her.[30]

In 2012, there were a slew of gang rape cases: McGill University, Presbyterian College, Old Dominion University, Naval Academy, the University of Texas, and Ohio State. 2013 was Vanderbilt and Brown.[31]

Two University of New Mexico players and another student were charged with kidnapping and raping another student in 2014, the players being suspended indefinitely from the team in response. The charges were dropped and the players returned to the team. That same year, two University of Miami players were charged with sexual battery after a woman reported that they had raped her. Two Texas players were arrested and charged after a female student said they raped her in a dorm room. Two Tennessee players were also charged with raping a woman.[32]

In total, of the 110-plus cases I have found, forty-nine of them (either accusations, charges, or convictions) involved multiple football players who allegedly participated directly in the sexual assault.

V.

So many of these cases are collective experiences. All of these cases that involve multiple players, either as participants, witnesses, or intimidators after the fact, seem to support Sanday's thesis that these acts of sexual violence are as much about bonding between men as anything else. They also suggest that it is necessary to take a long, critical look at the culture of football teams and the famous mystique of the locker room.

There are a few cases where there are witnesses to the violence. For example, in 2013, a man at Hobart and William Smith Colleges lost track of his friend at a party. "He found her," he told the *New York Times* in 2014, "bent over a pool table as a football player appeared to be sexually assaulting her from behind in a darkened dance hall with six or seven people watching and laughing. Some had their cell phones out, apparently taking pictures, he said." The university cleared the players within twelve days. At Vanderbilt that same year, while four players were charged with raping a woman, at least four other student-athletes testified to seeing the woman that night and two helped move her body at one point into the room of one of the defendants from the hallway.[33]

Women who come forward to report being assaulted can face intense harassment, sometimes at the hands of the player's teammates. In 1984, when charges were dismissed against a University of Florida player, the woman in the case told the local paper that she had been harassed by teammates of his and this played a role in her choosing not to testify. In 1991, Kathy Redmond, founder of National Coalition Against Violent Athletes, was a student at Nebraska when she reported that Christian Peter, a nose tackle on the football team, raped her twice two years earlier (the second time with two of his teammates standing guard at the door). Peter would later be found guilty of sexually assaulting a different woman, but he denies that he raped Redmond. She has said that after she came forward, she received death threats, prank phone calls, and her car was vandalized. A woman who reported being raped by a Michigan player in 2009 also reported receiving rape threats from one of the player's teammates. In 2010, Lizzy Seeberg reported being sexually assaulted by a Notre Dame player. The next day, her parents say, she received a disturbing text message from a friend of the player that read, *Don't do anything you'd regret. Messing with Notre Dame football is a bad idea.* Not long after, Seeberg committed suicide.[34]

In all, just over 40 percent of the cases I've studied are gang rape allegations involving multiple players. If you add in cases where teammates are witnesses or later accomplices in harassing the woman who reported the violence, it creeps up close to 50 percent. This is incredibly high compared to what is known about gang rapes in the overall population. In 2013, Sarah E. Ullman wrote in a book about multiple-perpetrator rape that research provides a wide range of possibilities for how common gang rape is: "From under 2 percent in student populations to up to 26 percent in police-reported cases."[35] Granted, my research is unscientific and limited by my access to resources, but even if I am off by 10-plus percentage points, the rate of gang behavior in these cases is remarkable.

VI.

Other patterns suggest systemic issues that go beyond the confines of individual teams. Plenty of players, even if dismissed by their team or university, transfer schools. That move, of transferring after being accused of sexual violence, goes back to the earliest case I could locate: one of the six players accused of raping the woman at Notre Dame in 1974 transferred. It was true for a player at Arkansas in 1992 who went to Sonoma State after being dismissed. It happened again at Notre Dame in 1997, when the school expelled a player after a disciplinary hearing found him guilty of violating the school's conduct code. He transferred to West Virginia. And again at Notre Dame in 2002: the player who pleaded guilty to sexual battery transferred to Kent State and eventually played for the New York Jets. In 2007, two Iowa players, one who was convicted of misdemeanor assault and the other who pleaded guilty to an assault charge, both transferred schools. Three Minnesota players accused in 2007 transferred to Cincinnati, Kentucky State, and Illinois State. A Missouri player was sentenced to five years in prison for sexually assaulting a fellow student, served only 120 days, and then transferred to Tuskegee. The two Vanderbilt players from the 2013 gang rape who still await trial both transferred to other schools.[36]

I'm not suggesting that players not be allowed to transfer, but more pointing out that there is no mechanism in place that holds anyone accountable. NCAA rules require athletes who change schools following disqualifications or suspensions for "disciplinary reasons" to sit out a year before being eligible to compete, but do not impose stricter standards or outright bans on athletes suspended or disqualified for sexual assault. Moreover, the one-year sit-out is often skirted using a one-time transfer exception available to almost all athletes, except those in revenue-producing sports (and even those athletes can use the exception if they drop down a division).

"If a student is charged with sexual assault, or even found responsible in a university system, there is nothing to keep that individual from transferring to another school," says a representative from End Rape on Campus, an organization that has helped many people file Title IX lawsuits with the Department of Education asking for investigations into how their universities have handled sexual assault allegations.[37] "Basically," they tell me, "this means rapists can transfer freely, and commit the same crime with the only penalty being a completely new pool of victims at a different school."

Much like schools in general, campus athletic departments are under no obligation to review athlete disciplinary records before accepting transfers. And even when athletic officials are aware of someone's troubled past, many look the other way. A wide receiver left Missouri for Oklahoma in 2014 after being dismissed from the school's football team following an incident in which he pushed a woman down a flight of stairs. In 2013, a Providence basketball player was accused of sexually assaulting a fellow student and was "prohibited from participating in games for the rest of the season." He transferred to Oregon, where he was eventually expelled with two other players after an accusation of gang rape. He played the 2014–15 season at Northwestern Florida State College, where school president Ty Handy said the player will have a chance to "succeed, to grow, and to develop."[38]

Coaches also leave behind the mess of these cases and any potential fallout. Mike Riley left Oregon State in 1998 after a season in which multiple players were accused of raping a student. He headed to the San Diego Chargers, had a brief stint with the Saints, and returned to OSU from 2003–2014. He is now at Nebraska. Mack Brown, the famed coach at the University of Texas, saw two of his players reported for sexual assault in 2012. Both remained on the team when no charges were pressed. A year later, Brown retired. Within six months, two more players from the team were arrested for sexual assault and the new head coach, Charlie Strong, dismissed them. James Franklin, head coach of Vanderbilt when four players were arrested in the summer of 2013, left the school the following January and now is head coach at Penn State. In a pretrial hearing before two of the players went to court, Franklin had to Skype in to give testimony and answer questions.[39]

Problems with the criminal justice system reverberate out into the decisions coaches and teams make about these players. Many of the cases end with dismissed charges due to inadequate evidence or the woman who initially reported the crime backing out. Both are common to cases involving interpersonal or sexual violence, though when athletes are the ones named as perpetrators, the stakes get much higher for everyone involved, including law enforcement, prosecutors, and the woman herself. (Note: men are the victims of sexual assault too, but it is so rare to find a man who publicly reports his rape at the hand of an athlete, and those incidents are often reported not as sexual assault but rather as hazing, so they get lost in searches for this kind of violence.)

For cases that did make it past the arrest phase, many were pleaded out to reduced charges and the players received light sentences. That is ridiculously common, regardless of the case. According to the *New York Review of Books*, "In 2013, while 8 percent of all federal criminal charges were dismissed (either because of a mistake in fact or law or because the defendant had decided to cooperate), more than 97 percent of the remainder were resolved through plea bargains, and fewer than 3 percent went to trial. The plea bargains largely determined the sentences imposed."[40] At the state level, "it is a rare state where plea bargains do not similarly account for the resolution of at least 95 percent of the felony cases that are not dismissed."

Coaches often look to legal outcomes to decide how to handle players who are accused. That is fine, as long as we acknowledge that legal outcomes in these cases are complicated and often do not resolve the cases in a manner that withdraws all doubt about the crime. Yes, legally, when a case is pleaded or a trial completed, there is a cut-and-dry answer for whether the defendant is innocent or guilty in the eyes of the law; in the rest of the world, however, the one outside of the courtroom, we are left to coexist with people whose legal innocence or guilt does not seem satisfying or fair. When a coach decides to give or deny a player a "second chance" based only on the legal outcome, that too can seem unsatisfying or unfair because of the troubles with the legal system itself.

VII.

Let's take one school as an example of how a case can appear isolated but often fits into a longer, larger history: Florida State.

Early in the morning on December 7, 2012, a Florida State University student called the FSU Police Department (FSUPD) and reported that her friend, Erica Kinsman, had been raped. (Kinsman has released her name publicly, hence its use in this book.[41])

Over the next twenty-four hours, Kinsman gave statements to multiple officers and went to the hospital for a rape kit. But she did not know the name of the man she said raped her. In mid-January, thirty-four days after Kinsman initially reported to the Tallahassee Police Department (TPD), Kinsman recognized the man she had reported on December 7 when they both showed up for a class in the new spring semester. She contacted the TPD on January 10, 2013, and told detective Scott Angulo that she now knew the man's name; it was Jameis Winston, she said.

"This case is being suspended at this time due to a lack of cooperation from the victim. If the victim decides to press

charges, the case will be pursued." Those two sentences conclude Angulo's February 11 TPD report. Angulo and his colleagues had not collected video from the bar where Winston
and the woman had met earlier in the night. They had failed
to find the cab driver who took the two of them, as well as
Winston's roommate Casher and another player, Ronald Darby,
back to Winston and Casher's apartment. They did not interview anyone other than Kinsman and two of her friends. They
did submit her rape kit, and both her blood and urine tested
negative for drugs. It wasn't until late August, though, that
the TPD received word that "semen was present on [her] anal
swabs, panties, and pink shorts (later verified to be pink pants)."
TPD never compelled Winston to provide his DNA for testing.

After the story broke on November 13, 2013, Winston
finally submitted his DNA for testing. It matched the DNA
from the rape kit. Winston, through his attorney, said it was
consensual sex. Kinsman's family, in response, released a statement saying, "To be clear, the victim did not consent. This was
a rape." The media, as they do, boiled the case down to a typical
he-said/she-said debate.

But the real story was the long string of failures. It quickly
became apparent that a full investigation was never done and
the state's attorney was never contacted to look into the case.
That office began its own investigation. Kinsman was once
again questioned, as were friends she had been with or whom
she'd contacted that night. On the same day that TPD first released a heavily redacted version of the initial police report, before police ever interviewed them, Winston's lawyer submitted
affidavits from Casher and Darby about what they remembered
from that night eleven months earlier. TPD also interviewed
them in the following days, when they found out that Casher
had recorded Winston and the woman in Winston's bedroom

but had since deleted the video and gotten rid of the phone. They both maintained that Winston was innocent and that Kinsman had consented.

Winston was never questioned by the police or the state attorney's office.

But Winston's case was not in isolation even at his own school: in June 2013, just over six months after Kinsman first reported to the police, FSU wide receiver Greg Dent was suspended indefinitely from the team after he was charged with second-degree sexual assault. A woman told police he was "very aggressive in touching" her and did eventually penetrate her before she fought him off. Dent was eventually found guilty in September 2014 of misdemeanor battery, not sexual battery. He was sentenced to time served and put on probation for six months. He hopes to return to the green grass of Doak Campbell Stadium after his probation is complete. When he heard the news about Dent only receiving a conviction for misdemeanor battery, Jimbo Fisher, FSU head coach, told the *Orlando Sentinel*, "I'm extremely happy for him that that turned out. I think Greg is an outstanding young man, always did, and you know, [the possibility of him returning] is out there. We'll address that when it comes, but I'm extremely happy for him." Adding that he had stayed in contact with Dent throughout the legal process, Fisher said, "Greg is one of our children and you have to be there and be very supportive." In March 2016, Dent returned to Florida State to participate in their annual pro day, to set himself up for a chance at getting on an NFL roster.

In the coverage of the case against Winston, there was almost no mention of Dent.

This is troubling because when the news broke about Winston, there were multiple pieces drawing attention to how football culture and rape culture both operate within Tallahassee and on FSU's campus. Stassa Edwards wrote at *Ms. Magazine's* blog in November 2013 that "the town has gone mad, spouting conspiracy theories that 'prove' Winston's innocence."[42] She said she overhead victim-blaming at a local Mexican restaurant in the city, a woman saying to her teenage daughter, "She's just ruining Jameis's good character." And Edwards charged that the local paper, the *Tallahassee Democrat*, was doing a poor job in covering the case. She said they were "pandering to some of the worst sensibilities of rape culture: the immediate need to suspect an accuser's intention and tear apart her story before we even have it."

"Here in Tallahassee, the victim-blaming is so overwhelming," Edwards wrote, "that the editor of a Gannett-owned newspaper can, the day after the story was reported, declare the evidence against Winston to be 'thin on the surface.'"

"Jameis Winston Isn't the Only Problem Here: An FSU Teacher's Lament" was the title of Adam Weinstein's *Deadspin* piece around that same time period.[43] Weinstein said he and his colleagues, while loving football, were "increasingly flummoxed by the football culture surrounding Tallahassee, one that's grown malignant with the wins and the scrutiny." That malignancy resulted in "most of Tallahassee, even the local sports reporters," not being able, Weinstein said, to "accept that the narrative [around FSU football] is overly simple, and that failure is always an option, whether it's a physical failure in the fourth quarter, or a moral one in a strange bedroom after last call on Tennessee Street." And so, like Edwards, Weinstein chronicles the vast range of theories people created to explain away the possibility that Winston had raped someone and why no one bothered to adequately investigate it:

It's the timing of this thing going public—some Manziel

or McCarron fan dropping a bomb before Heisman vot-
ing, before BCS selection. Maybe even a (voice drops to a
whisper) Gators fan. It's the height of discrepancy in the
police report—and that chick doesn't know what the hell
went on, probably because she was drinking. It's some ly-
ing jealous gold-digger. It's racism. It's a state attorney who
is grandstanding or maybe corrupt or maybe just has a
hard-on for unfairly persecuting football players for rape.

"The detective I spoke to said, 'Are you sure you want to pursue this? It's been three months, so it's just he-said/she-said at this point. That doesn't usually go well.'" That was Marci Robin's experience with the Tallahassee police when she reported her rape in 1999 while a student at FSU.[44] She wrote about it in November 2013 for *xoJane*. "I told them I just knew I needed to report it: It happened, here's his name, here's my account, please do something. Nothing." Robin said she told her story because it was eerily similar to what Kinsman said had happened to her when she reported her rape. For Kinsman, though, there was the added layer of reporting a star player at a university and in a town obsessed with football.

Florida State football's history of players being accused and/or charged with sexual crimes, from harassment to rape, goes back to at least the mid-1990s. Months after kicking the winning field goal in the Orange Bowl against Nebraska, a win that secured FSU's national championship for the 1993 season, Scott Bentley pleaded no contest to charges that he illegally taped a Florida A&M student while the two were having consensual sex. He later played the tape for his friends, some of them his teammates. He received forty hours of community service and a $500 fine. He said his reason for the recording was because he didn't trust the woman he was with. "I was protecting myself against potential false allegations that could be brought up in the future," Bentley told local news.[45] He was suspended for that summer, and allowed to return to the team a week before the start of training camp. Bentley went on to play multiple seasons in the NFL.

That same year, only a month later, Kamari Charlton, a tight end, was arrested after he was charged with one count each of sexual battery and battery.[46] His ex-girlfriend reported that he had raped her and grabbed her throat. Charlton was suspended and then dismissed from the team. He was later acquitted and returned to the team the following year.

Just before Christmas in 1993, former Florida State running back Michael Gibson burst into Ashley Witherspoon's apartment early in the morning. According to what she told *Deadspin* in April 2014, "We struggled. I was shot twice at point-blank range."[47] But then, she says, "What I've never gotten over, never been able to stomach, is that at that point, after shooting me, he made me lie down on the bed and raped me." Gibson was convicted and received six life sentences, one of them being for attempted felony murder. In 2003, when the Florida Supreme Court determined that "attempted felony murder" was not a crime, there was a sentencing hearing. Bobby Bowden wrote a letter of reference for Gibson in which he said Gibson was "no problem" while he was on the team. Witherspoon says, "The thing that sticks in my craw is that he signed the letter 'Coach Bowden,' as if we all wouldn't know who Bobby Bowden was. Who signs 'Coach Bowden' unless you're signing a poster or a football?"

The same year that Bowden penned that letter for Gibson, Travis Johnson, an FSU nose guard, was accused by a fellow FSU athlete and his former girlfriend of rape. According to the *Orlando Sentinel*, "Johnson's lawyers said the sexual encounter was consensual and that his accuser became angry when she learned Johnson had another girlfriend."[48] This case was particularly strange. The president of FSU at the time, T.K. Wetherell, spoke to both parties involved, which, the paper said, "FSU officials acknowledged . . . was unprecedented, as was Student Affairs Vice President Mary Coburn's attempt to mediate [an] agreement before the criminal matter was resolved." Coburn apparently asked the woman to drop the charges in exchange for Johnson going to counseling and leaving school for six months, which would have brought him back to campus in time for the start of the next year's football season. The woman declined Coburn's plan. The case went all the way to court, and Johnson was acquitted after only thirty minutes of deliberation. In November 2013, according to Johnson, "he passed three polygraph examinations and that two medical experts told investigators the attack was unlikely to have happened the way the complainant described." He went on to play six seasons in the NFL.

In November 2015, late on the Wednesday before Thanksgiving, Florida State released court documents to the *New York Times*.[49] Included was the deposition of the former director of FSU's Victim Advocate Office. Her testimony is part of Kinsman's civil suit against Winston. According to the *Times*, "In the nine years she worked in that office, an estimated forty football players had been accused of either sexual assault or 'intimate partner' violence, and that to the best of her recollection, only one person had been found responsible. She said most of the women chose not to pursue the cases 'based on fear.' No names were mentioned." When the *Times* asked FSU for a response to the former director's testimony, the school released a statement saying, "We have no way to confirm or deny Ms. Ashton's claims, given that her communications with such victims are confidential."

VIII.

There is no isolated case when we talk about college football and sexual assault.

My alma mater, Florida State, has a history of problems when it comes to football players and sexual violence. Many of these cases are more clear now that journalists and a civil suit have unearthed this information due to the level of scrutiny the Winston case brought on the school.

The takeaway cannot be that Florida State is an anomaly, though. It is an example of the ordinary.

When we adopt routine responses to individual cases, it's important to remember that this is a playing field. Recognizing that each case is part of a long-standing problem that has affected many people at different schools for decades now means that we can and should shift away from the narrow lens of obsessing over single cases.

Let's broaden the conversation to one that tries to understand the overarching systems of power that inform how these cases are handled, how they are discussed, and ultimately why nothing about them ever seems to change.

What the Playbook Doesn't Show

I.

When you look at a single play in a playbook, it is usually fairly simple in design. It is sketched with lines, arrows, and symbols that indicate what each position is supposed to do, and there is often a short explanation, sometimes as few as three words, that describes the movement in more detail. What goes without saying is that the play is sketched out on a football field. That is a given. Where else, in fact, would those plays happen?

In the current playbook about college football and sexual assault, the things not said, the things that are taken for granted, the things that are simply known, are the racial and gendered hierarchies that inform how we think about these cases. In our society, there is a reason cases involving African American players garner more attention than those of white ones. We are trained to see black men as perpetrators who need to be punished and controlled by the state. We also believe women to be dramatic and/or liars when they share their experiences, especially their interactions with men. No one needs to tell us these things each time a new college case breaks, before we hear any evidence or analysis. Who else would commit such a crime, if not young black men? Who else would lie about having sex after the fact, if not young women?

The given in this playbook is that the intersection of race,

gender, and money matters deeply to understanding the intersection of college football and sexual assault. It goes without
saying because we already know it. But it shouldn't go without
saying because, while we focus on the black-man-as-criminal
and the woman-as-liar, what is lost is that most of the people who create and maintain the culture of college football are
white men, from coaches to athletic directors, from university
presidents to the media who cover the sport. And all those
white men make a lot of money off the backs of the players and
they have no problem hushing up the voices of mainly women
when they feel those women could threaten their players, their
game, and their money.

This chapter is the discussion of what we so rarely say. This
topic has to be discussed with the utmost care, though, in a
country that likes to so easily criminalize and stigmatize black
men, and so readily deems women as untrustworthy.

II.

I remember Travis Johnson. Our time at Florida State as un-
dergraduates overlapped and there was one semester where we
shared a class. I knew he was a football player. There were a
handful in the class and our teacher, a large, jovial graduate student in the classics department, seemed smitten with the idea
that he was sharing space with these campus rock stars. I was
too. I never directly interacted with Johnson (there were probably fifty to seventy students in the class) but my memory of him
is one of a loud goofball, the class clown. During the middle of
an exam, the room silent as pencils scratched on paper, Johnson, seemingly out of nowhere, yelled, "Sexual chocolate!" The
room erupted in laughter, a huge smile broke across his face, the
instructor shushed us, and we went back to our work.

Johnson was also a big black man in small Southern town.

In April 2003, a year after I graduated from FSU, Johnson was charged with sexual battery and suspended from the team.[50] The woman who reported the assault was a shot-putter on the FSU track team and had a prior relationship with Johnson. She said that in early February that year, Johnson took her to another player's apartment, held her there against her will, and raped her. She then reported it to a coach and twelve days later to the police. At trial, according to the *St. Petersburg Times*, the woman said she waited because "I was embarrassed, and I wanted him to leave me alone," and, the paper says, "she also didn't want to 'ruin' Johnson."[51]

Nine days after the woman reported to law enforcement, Mary Coburn, the university's Student Affairs vice president, sent her an e-mail. The *Orlando Sentinel* published that e-mail:

> *"Even though Travis does not admit this wrongdoing, to avoid embarrassment to himself, his family, the university, and you, Travis has agreed to withdraw from spring semester and not return until August 8 which is football reporting day. He has also agreed to receive counseling and provide documentation to me that this has taken place."* The e-mail also stipulated that *"all parties agree to keep this matter confidential"* and *"not pursue any further legal action."*[52]

It appears that Coburn attempted to make the case go away, and she tried to do it around the football schedule to make sure that the team's starting defensive tackle didn't miss a game. Football is big business.

Three days later, the woman pressed charges.

Johnson maintained throughout the investigation and eventual trial that it was consensual sex and that he, having had shoulder surgery weeks earlier and the woman being only slightly smaller than him, could not have raped her.

Willie Meggs, the state attorney, took the case to court. The trial lasted two days, Johnson did not testify, the woman was on the stand for three hours, and it took the six women who made up the jury thirty minutes to find him not guilty. The *Sun-Sentinel* reported at the time that the woman and her family, as well as Johnson and his family, cried after the verdict was read.[53] Afterward, Johnson's attorney said the fact that "this case was even brought this far is troubling."[54] Johnson played for FSU the next season and was drafted into the NFL in 2005, where he played for six years.

When news broke in November 2013 that Willie Meggs's office was investigating Jameis Winston, Travis Johnson emerged as a vocal critic of the state attorney. Johnson tweeted repeatedly about Meggs throughout November and into December. He called Meggs "the most Racist&Biased individual" and "the Most Corrupt Criminal in all of Florida." "Willie Meggs will never give anyone let alone a black man a fair shake in the state of flordia he is a media hoe," read one tweet. He also told *Yahoo! Sports*, "Facts don't matter when you are dealing with a guy like Willie Meggs. Willie Meggs isn't out for the facts . . . At the end of the day, this is still the Jim Crow South. You think, 'It's Florida.' Well, it's not Florida. It's South Georgia. Tallahassee is South Georgia."

Tallahassee is only a twenty-minute drive from the border with Georgia, and much of what surrounds it is rural. The refrain that it is really *southern* Georgia was one I heard while attending school. The county votes Democrat generally, but often with close margins. And, like most cities in the US South, it has a history saturated with segregation and racism.[55] Tallahassee was the site of a seven-month boycott of city buses in

1956 after two black women were arrested for sitting beside a white woman. The KKK held rallies in the city and burned crosses from the 1940s on. Young black people in the 1960s and 1970s held sit-ins, picketed segregated businesses, and marched through the city.

The past is never left in the past, though. There are ongoing arguments about the school's mascot, the Seminoles, which has a red-faced man in profile as its main symbol. A social media post at the start of the school year in 2013 referred to black FSU students as "monkeys," sparking justified outrage and a university investigation. The following year, a lecturer who had been with the university for eighteen years quit after her racist Facebook rant went public. In late 2014, multiple black churches in the rural area around Tallahassee were vandalized within a week of one another.[56] On March 18, 2015, the local paper, the *Tallahassee Democrat,* reported that the KKK had distributed leaflets in the city.[57] "Imperial Wizard of the Traditionalist American Knights of the Ku Klux Klan Frank Ancona said the fliers found in Tallahassee driveways over the past few days were an effort to spread awareness of the values the organization holds and hopefully draw in new members." In December 2015, a black student at Florida State wrote a letter to the president of FSU, John Thrasher, after Thrasher's State of the University address.[58] After a long, detailed list of issues of discrimination and racism at FSU and within the state of Florida more generally, the student wrote, "Acts of racism and intolerance are not, as you claim, 'isolated acts' at Florida State; they are the culmination and furtherance of ideals this university has perpetuated for decades." All of this is probably what Travis Johnson meant when he said that Tallahassee is "still the Jim Crow South."

As evidence of Meggs's particular interest in football players, people often point to a 2003 interview he gave to the

Sun-Sentinel where he said, "To whom much is given, much should be expected. Sometimes we ought to hold those folks to a little bit higher standard. Thousands of people would give their right arm to play for FSU or Notre Dame or Miami or Georgia, and when somebody messes up doing something stupid, it's a shame."[59] The idea that FSU football players are given much is questionable. There is also an implication in the phrase "hold to a higher standard" that the people Meggs is talking about should be brought down a peg. Those can be loaded words in a Southern town in northern Florida, especially when spoken by a white man about mainly black men.

Also, it is not just football players who maintain that race plays a role in how Meggs practices law. In February 2012, Leon County Commissioner Bill Proctor said Meggs "just beats the hell out of black folk day in and day out," prosecuting them at higher rates. In a press release, Proctor wrote that Meggs "prosecutes black officials with great haste and fervor but is hesitant and indifferent to white public officials who commit crimes."

Willie Meggs might be racist in how he practices law, as Proctor and Johnson say. He might not. In the end, it ultimately may not matter because Meggs, a white Southern man who is an agent of the state, practices law in a system that many feel is racist in whom it labels as criminal and how it punishes them.

III.

This country has a long history of tying blackness to criminality (and vice versa) in ways that have devastating effects in real life: "African Americans make up 13 percent of the general US population, yet they constitute 28 percent of all arrests, 40 percent of all inmates held in prisons and jails, and 42 percent of the population on death row."[60] What this means is that we find it easier to talk about crime, especially crime as a problem within our larger society, when we have an African American in the role of perpetrator.

In 2014 I met up with Ben Carrington, a professor of sociology at the University of Texas who specializes in sports and race, at a swanky coffee shop in downtown Austin to talk to him about this. Carrington, a native Londoner with a smooth English accent and himself a former semipro footballer in Europe, told me that often "race is the trigger for society to express their moral outrage about another issue." (In this case, sexual violence.) In fact, he said, when a crime is perpetrated by black people, that "helps to make us more angry because of what [the alleged perpetrators] look like." Football, Carrington noted, because it employs so many black men and is so popular, reflects a skewed racialized image of violence back into our society. We care about football a lot, we pay attention to what the players do on and off the field, we critique their behavior on and off the field, and when black players are accused, charged, or convicted of criminal behavior, it slots nicely into our cultural imagination regarding black men.

Other experts echo Carrington's concerns. In September 2014, while working on a piece about how the NFL was handling a slew of domestic violence accusations and charges against its players, all of whom happened to be black, I spoke to Mariame Kaba on the phone.[61] Based in Chicago, Kaba is an antiviolence organizer who founded the Chicago Taskforce on Violence Against Girls & Young Women. Her work is not about sports but rather about violence. She echoed Carrington's points, telling me she's "dubious to the reaction to [these cases] versus the reaction to white [players] who commit violence," because when it is black men we are discussing, there are implications of these men being "inherently violent," and that makes for an easy leap to saying "they should be locked up, we need to manage and control them." This is particularly true when the crime is sexual assault.

I then called up Louis Moore, a professor of history at Grand Valley State University, to talk about a historical phenomenon that he called "black men as the natural rapist." Moore told me, "If you just look up 'negro' and 'lynched' in any kind of history database, most of the time [the lynching was justified by] an accusation of rape never founded because there was no due process." What this means, Moore said, is that in all discussions of rape culture in the US, no matter how far back you go in history, "race is always forefront of the conversation just because of the history of race and alleged rape in America." A paucity of black men on many campuses feeds into an image that they are outliers in the community. People "think they are on campus for two reasons," Moore said, "affirmative action or athletics. So there is this sense that they don't belong, sense that they never belonged, and when the crime happens it becomes, 'See, I told you so.'"

This is all heightened when we talk about black male athletes in particular. Carrington told me that he traces the outlier status of black athletes within sports, even when they are a numerical majority, to the history of integration of sports in this country. He says that black athletes—ever since Jack Johnson became the first black heavyweight champion in 1908—have been painted as "angry, rebellious, violent, uncontrollable."

This is further troubled when talking about cases where a black athlete is reported to have raped a white woman. The lynchings that Moore mentioned were often justified under the racialized and paternalistic gendered scare tactic of saying that the women these angry, rebellious, violent, uncontrollable natural rapists attacked were white. That horrific part of US history and the ongoing racial disparities within the criminal justice system mean that accusations of black men sexually assaulting white women carry within them additional cultural baggage that has to, at the least, be acknowledged in these conversations. Fears about powerful black men being punished via false accusation are not irrational or dramatic; they are borne of actual experience.

In cases where people do not know the race of the accuser, it's often assumed that it is a white woman. (This narrative, it should be noted, erases and ignores black female victims, which is an ongoing issue within these conversations as well as in victim-centered antiviolence campaigns.)

Lisa Lindquist Dorr studied the history of the myth of black men raping white women in *White Women, Rape, and the Power of Race in Virginia, 1900–1960*.[62] This narrative enforced, Dorr argues, a racist and sexist system of power by reifying "white women's subordination to white men and the social, economic, and political power of whites over blacks." In the complicated gendered and racialized postslavery South, white men were in control of everyone else; the appearance of protecting white women from black men helped cement that reality.

The system of power that gave that myth force is still with us. In June 2015, after Dylann Storm Roof reportedly said, "You rape our women, and you're taking over our country, and you have to go," before murdering nine black people in a historically black church in Charleston, South Carolina, Jamelle Bouie wrote succinctly, "Make any list of anti-black terrorism in the United States, and you'll also have a list of attacks justified by the specter of black rape."[63] From Emmett Till to the Central Park Five, the history of young black men wrongly accused or convicted of harassing or raping white women is ever-present. Till was just fourteen in 1955 when a group of white men in Money, Mississippi, brutally mutilated him before killing him, supposedly because he spoke with a white woman and maybe whistled at her. Decades later, the Central Park Five were four young black men and one young Latino who were arrested and charged with the rape and assault of a white female jogger in Central Park in 1989. After coercive interrogations by the police, they each confessed to some part of the crime and were convicted and sent to jail. Just over a decade later, another man confessed to the crime and DNA evidence supported his account. The convictions for the five were vacated in 2002, though each had already served his sentence.

A 2012 study by Samuel Gross and Michael Shaffer from the University of Michigan School of Law looked at 873 exonerations in the United States between 1989 and 2012.[64] They found that race did play a significant role in exonerations in sexual assault cases: while 25 percent of prisoners convicted of sexual assault were black, African American men made up 63 percent of the exonerations in these cases. And of all those exonerations of black men, nearly three-quarters involved a white victim. The reason for this, they found, is not malicious lying but rather eyewitness misidentifications. Gross and Shaffer say that for rape cases, "The false convictions we know about are overwhelmingly caused by mistaken eyewitness identifications—a problem that is almost entirely restricted to crimes committed by strangers."

Additionally, Shaffer and Gross found that rape, compared to other crimes (except robbery), has the lowest rate of people lying and it leading to false convictions. Perjury and false accusations led to 64 percent of homicide exonerations, 74 percent of child sex abuse exonerations, 43 percent for other violent crimes, and 52 percent for exonerations of nonviolent crimes. Looking at all 873 exonerations cases, half were due to perjury or false accusations. When it came to sexual assault cases, that number was only 23 percent. In other words, compared to other types of crime, people who report rape are much less likely to lie.

In the end, this is what the study tells us: it is both a myth that black men rape white women at some extraordinary level and that women lie profusely to falsely convict men. Yet the system, as it is set up, seems to suggest both things are true. Many people in this society believe these things to be true.

This is a particularly damaging intersection of racism and sexism, then, for both women and black men. As Byron Hurt wrote on December 5, 2013, in a piece for *NewBlackMan (in Exile)* about the Jameis Winston case, "It is true that Black men continue to be cruelly stereotyped as rapists. As a Black man, I carry that label—and all of the other stereotypes associated with Black men—wherever I go in our country. However, it is also a stereotype that women lie about being victims of rape more often than not. According to FBI statistics, less than 3 percent of all rapes are falsely reported."[65]

Yet the exoneration study shows that false convictions for rape are most likely made when the woman does not know her perpetrator and when there is a mistake in his identification; it is not done with malicious intent. That does not mean the woman is not racist or that because the intent is not malicious that the effects of a racist system do not have terrible real-life consequences for black men.

It's important to note one potential horrific consequence for men behind bars, whether they committed a crime or not: they can become victims of sexual violence themselves as prison rape is at crisis levels in the United States. According to Elizabeth Stoker Bruenig, the data from the Bureau of Justice Statistics indicates that "a prisoner's likelihood of becoming a victim of sexual assault is roughly thirty times higher than that of any given woman on the outside" and "inmates in state and federal prisons and local jails all reported greater rates of sexual victim-ization involving staff than other inmates."[66] Kirsten West Savali has argued that ignoring prison rape further marginalizes the struggle to get people to care about mitigating or ending sex-ual violence altogether.[67] "Until we create safe spaces for these victims, for *all* victims, to be truly seen and heard," West Savali writes, "rape culture will continue to be viewed as a 'woman's problem' or a 'man-hating, feminist agenda'—something soci-ety has always found easy to deny or vilify, and ultimately ig-nore." These things are complicated issues: racism in the system and in our daily lives means that more black men are criminal-ized overall and are often misidentified in criminal prosecutions of sexual assault cases; they then go into a prison system where they very well may become victims of sexual violence them-selves; and by us ignoring the issue of prison rape (probably because we believe it is a justified punishment or because we simply do not care about what happens to the population of people behind bars), we continue to perpetuate the very rape culture we say we want to end.

In college football, many (though not all) of the sexual assault cases involving college players fall outside of the "stranger dan-ger" rape scenario that leads to misidentification of the perpe-trator and so to false convictions. Most of the time, the woman knows the man she is reporting. Additionally, many of these cases involve gang rapes by multiple players (roughly 40 per-cent), a scenario that does not lend itself to overarching prob-lems with eyewitnesses misidentifying perpetrators. This does not mean that race and racist beliefs about black men's crimi-nality have no place in these cases, only that most of these cases are more complicated than our nuance-averse narratives allow.

There is no way to determine with 100 percent certainty that the person reporting the crime is telling the truth. Yet the statistical odds are very high that the person reporting in these cases is not lying. Still, we have to also hold in our minds that race does play a role, clearly, in false rape convictions.

One other area where race most definitely has an impact is our appetite for consuming crime reportage when the person accused, charged, or convicted is a black athlete. We find it easy to talk about crime, especially crime as a problem within our larger society, when we have a black person in the role of perpetrator.

IV.

Willie Meggs, the prosecutor who took Travis Johnson to court, was the same state attorney in charge of Jameis Winston's case in 2013. In the end, Meggs chose not to press charges against Winston. What he did, though, was take the opportunity to make the announcement of not charging Winston into a spectacle. He laughed multiple times during the press conference. At one point, Meggs was on screen standing behind a podium, and a female reporter off camera asked him, "Because there was more than one DNA evidence in the rape kit, can you conclude that there was perhaps sex with more than one male?" Meggs paused and then replied, "That would be a logical conclusion." The man standing just behind him on camera, former Florida state senator Alfred Lawson, laughed in response, as did other people in the room. That was toward the beginning of the strangely lighthearted press conference about a high-profile sexual assault case. Meggs repeatedly cracked jokes with the media. When asked if the deadline for Heisman voting influenced how quickly or when Meggs determined that he would not press charges, he jokingly asked when the voting ended and then smirked while saying it did not affect his timeline. Then Meggs and Lawson kidded about whether Lawson had called him a "politician," leading Meggs to grin widely for the camera, seemingly pleased with his own humor.

Ashley Witherspoon, who was shot and raped in 1993 by a former FSU football player, Michael Gibson, while a student at FSU, told *Deadspin* in April 2014 that "Willie Meggs was my attorney. He was a bulldog. I felt like he was going to help protect me and make it right."[68] He did. Gibson is serving five life sentences. But Witherspoon was dismayed after Meggs's press conference, saying, "When I had dealings with Meggs, he was a protector. He was incredibly invested in my trial. Hardcore. So to hear that he could laugh and not take it seriously, so it became a media joke session—it hurt me. That wasn't the Willie Meggs I knew. He was my knight in shining armor way back when. That luster is gone."

The controversies that surround Willie Meggs are a stark reminder of the fact that the racist system that overcriminalizes black men is the same sexist one that does a poor job handling cases of sexual violence. Both make talking about college football and sexual violence a difficult, complex topic. The least we can do is not laugh about it.

V.

Alongside the troubled history of race and sexual violence is this country's long and ongoing history of exploiting the bodies of black people for their labor. We now see these issues playing out with regard to college athletics, especially around football and basketball, sports dominated by black athletes.

When I spoke to Louis Moore, he emphasized to me what universities and athletic departments are actually concerned about. "When we talk about the college athlete, we have to remember this is a source of free labor. So [universities] are reluctant to do anything about [problems involving their athletes].

Their position is more the color green than the color black."

The "green" Moore is referring to is the lucrative amount of money that flows through the college football system. In December 2014, the Department of Education said that the revenue for the sport was roughly $3.4 billion, an incredible number.[69] ESPN alone pays billions of dollars to broadcast the games. Schools and the NCAA generate money from TV rights, merchandise sales, ticket sales, concessions at games, etc. *USA Today* reported in January 2016 that the SEC conference made "$527.4 million in total revenue for a fiscal year that ended August 31, 2015. That was the first fiscal year in which the conference began receiving money from the formation of the SEC Network and from the new College Football Playoff."[70] The Texas Longhorns were the most valuable football team in 2015, at $152 million, according to *Forbes*.[71] Notre Dame was second at $127 million and Tennessee third at $121 million. The highest-paid football coaches in 2015 were Nick Saban at Alabama and Jim Harbaugh at Michigan, who made upward of $7 million.[72] Ohio State's Urban Meyer pocketed $5.8 million, Oklahoma's Bob Stoops $5.4 million, and Florida State's Jimbo Fisher $5.1 million. David Williams at Vanderbilt is the highest-paid athletic director in the country, his annual paycheck topping out over $3 million.[73] Louisville's Tom Jurich makes $1.4 million and Florida's Jeremy Foley brings in $1.2 million. University presidents made an average of $400,000 in 2012.[74] The president of the NCAA pulled down $1.7 million, also in 2012.[75] It pays to be associated with a university and their football program.

The irony of all this is that athletic departments struggle to profit. The *Washington Post* found that "many departments also are losing more money than ever, as athletic directors choose to outspend rising income to compete in an arms race that is costing many of the nation's largest publicly funded universities and students millions of dollars."[76] And while schools struggle to match expenses to income, "the sports programs in these five conferences—the Big Ten, Big 12, Pacific-12, Southeastern Conference, and Atlantic Coast Conference—are the wealthiest in the country, and they are wealthy because of football."

That's the green. The other color? White. Most college football coaches, athletic directors, university presidents, and NCAA administrators are white, the vast majority of them male. In April 2015, Sally Jenkins wrote,

> *The NCAA just spent a week floating airy platitudes about inclusiveness vs. discrimination at the NCAA tournament in full shameless view of the public over a potentially discriminatory Indiana law. Yet no one in the candor-flinching organization so much as skipped a shrimp buffet or returned a gift bag in a fit of social conscience over the fact that 87.7 percent of its Division I athletic directors are white. Or that 90 percent of them are men. Meanwhile, just 22 percent of college basketball coaches are black, and the hiring of female coaches is plummeting across all sports.*[77]

She went on to note that the NCAA "trails every professional sports league in hiring diversity. Racially, it's dead last. In hiring women—get this—it's tied for last with the NFL." There is even more. "Yet 88 percent of presidents of the 126 universities in the Football Bowl Subdivision are white," Jenkins writes. "The coaches they hire are 88.9 percent white. Their NCAA faculty representatives are 93 percent white. And almost 100 percent of their Division I conference commissioners, 29 of 30, are white."

When it comes to players, though, the color is black. "Between 2007 and 2010, black men were 2.8 percent of full-time, degree-seeking undergraduate students, but 57.1 percent of football teams and 64.3 percent of basketball teams." This is one of the many findings of the 2013 study "Black Male Student-Athletes and Racial Inequalities in NCAA Division I College Sports."[78] In short, black men are dramatically overrepresented in the makeup of collegiate football teams as compared to the percentage of the study body they comprise. This matters deeply when we talk about money in college football.

In December 2015, the *Washington Post* published the results of "a survey of opinions on 'pay for play' policies" which found that "negative racial views about blacks were the single most important predictor of white opposition to paying college athletes." In other words, "The more negatively a white respondent felt about blacks, the more they opposed paying college athletes." The discussion around paying college athletes, then, "is implicitly a discussion about race." The continued effort to justify away why players are not paid while they destroy their bodies and bring in large sums of money is all tied up in our ideas about black men providing cheap or even free labor.

In a much-lauded piece at *Jacobin* in November 2014, NBA legend Kareem Abdul-Jabbar argued that "life for student-athletes is no longer the quaint Americana fantasy of the homecoming bonfire and a celebration at the malt shop. It's big business in which everyone is making money—everyone except the eighteen- to twenty-one-year-old kids who every game risk permanent career-ending injuries."[79] Abdul-Jabbar stated emphatically, "In the name of fairness, we must bring an end to the indentured servitude of college athletes and start paying them what they are worth."

Part of what this former basketball star does so well in his article is to counter most of the claims made about how cushy the life of a student-athlete on scholarship really is. He notes that "college athletes on scholarship are not allowed to earn money beyond the scholarship," unlike non-athlete students, that players risk injury to their bodies which can leave them without scholarship and with hefty medical bills, and all while "the millionaire coaches are allowed to go out and earn extra money outside their contracts. Many do, acquiring hundreds of thousands of dollars a year beyond their already enormous salaries."

The most common refrain about not paying these athletes who are at the center of millions and millions of dollars is that they are being compensated via their scholarships which will end in them gaining an education, if nothing else. But schools often let down student-athletes, especially black ones. In January 2015, two former University of North Carolina athletes, a football player and women's basketball player, sued the NCAA and the university for failing to provide the promised education about which we so often hear. The NCAA, the lawsuit read, "had ample warning, including empirical evidence from numerous academic experts, that many college athletes were not receiving a meaningful education, including—disproportionately—African American college athletes in revenue-producing sports." UNC, it turns out, had for nearly two decades created so-called "paper classes" that, per the name, only existed on paper in order to artificially boost the GPAs of student-athletes. The report that laid all of this out estimated that over 3,100 students benefited from this system in that time period. The lawsuit focused on the unequal impact this had on black students and found the reason for it all to be tied directly to greed, saying UNC and the NCAA

enjoyed a mutually beneficial relationship that neither

wished to disturb despite warning signs of academic fraud. The NCAA relished the exponential increase in revenue, which funded the NCAA's own operations and which was distributed to its member institutions. UNC likewise enjoyed the revenues that came with winning, as well as the increased popularity and attendant recruiting advantages.

The problem with the promised education for the black student-athlete, especially for athletes in high-profile, profit-generating sports, is also reflected in graduation rates. The 2013 study "Black Male Student-Athletes and Racial Inequalities in NCAA Division I College Sports" found that only 50 percent of black male athletes graduate within six years, which is a much lower rate than other student-athletes (67 percent), undergraduate students overall (73 percent), and black male undergraduate students overall (56 percent).[80] And knowing what we know now about UNC, it's impossible not to question the quality of education provided to the 50 percent of black male athletes who do graduate. The failed promise of education in exchange for making millions off of these men's labor seems patently unfair.

In his seminal article "The Shame of College Sports" for the *Atlantic* in 2011, Taylor Branch argued persuasively that "two of the noble principles on which the NCAA justifies its existence—'amateurism' and the 'student-athlete'—are cynical hoaxes, legalistic confections propagated by the universities so they can exploit the skills and fame of young athletes."[81] More pointedly, Branch wrote, "Big-time college sports are fully commercialized. Billions of dollars flow through them each year. The NCAA makes money, and enables universities and corporations to make money, from the unpaid labor of young athletes." And most famously, Branch said that "to survey the scene—corporations and universities enriching themselves on the backs of uncompensated young men, whose status as 'student-athletes' deprives them of the right to due process guaranteed by the Constitution—is to catch an unmistakable whiff of the plantation."

Exploitation is inherent in the system of college athletics; the humanity of players themselves is often stripped away by this kind of sports culture.

As Branch and Abdul-Jabbar argue, the NCAA (which is controlled by universities) participates in the commodification of athletes' bodies by refusing to allow universities to pay players for the work they do, while simultaneously making money itself off the backs of those players. They are teaching these players about exploitation and how to use other people's bodies for one's own ends.

These players and their bodies have often been "treated like objects or commodities" for others' consumption, says Heather Corinna, a sexuality activist and founder of *Scarleteen*, a site dedicated to providing sex education and resources to young adults. This can become a problem outside of just football when we think about how programs that are teaching these men about exploiting people also teach them that women exist for their pleasure and as potential prizes for choosing the right school to attend.

When recruits visit a university and are rewarded with access to women's bodies, Corinna says, whether it's in the form of sex partners or as eye candy, they probably understand the implicit messaging. The stripping away of the humanity of a woman by a potential rapist is similar in many ways—though not directly parallel—to the dehumanization that takes place when university administrators, team owners, and league commissioners commodify the bodies of these players.

The culture around (and therefore, the economy of) football today is dependent on a society that minimizes and/or ignores rape. It is the same culture that tells these men they are only as valued by what they can do on a football field. Those are two dangerous messages being handed down from above, from coaches, athletic directors, university administrators, and the NCAA.

VI.

Because the majority of high-profile athletes are black and we tend to pay attention when athletes are involved, the issue of campus sexual assault repeatedly has a black face on it. Black men, on many campuses, have become the face of a crime that they are demographically and statistically not the main perpetrators of.

The history of racial violence predicated largely on the fear that a black man has sexually violated a white woman, the statistics on mistaken identification in interracial crimes of sexual assault that lead to false imprisonment, the exploitation of black labor for the gain of (mainly) white men: these are all the things we don't seem to want to discuss each time a case involving a college football player comes to light. We already know about these realities in some way—if not explicitly, then through the osmosis that comes with being a part of a racist society. Alongside these issues, we hold closely our belief that women lie, exaggerate, or confuse their own recollections of personal experiences.

We have internalized these messages and we project them out onto the story whether we mean to or not. This is an unspoken aspect of the field that the plays in the playbook of sexual assault and college football are written upon. Who else would commit such a crime, if not young black men? Who else would lie about having sex after the fact, if not young women?

Our comfortable acceptance of the black football player as

perpetrator and the woman as liar can go without saying, and often does. When we focus on these two characters in our stories of assault, we aren't looking at everyone else. The white male head coaches, athletic directors, university presidents, members of the sports media, fans, NCAA employees, etc., are written out of the story, even though these men play important roles in the perpetuation of a culture that minimizes and sometimes even encourages sexual assault.

The rest of this book is less concerned with the football player and the victim. Instead, it will look at the people who often go unnoticed, the people who have drawn up and execute almost flawlessly their own plays in order to deflect responsibility for their role in the perpetuation of this violence.

Nothing to See Here

I.

So many of the plays that universities and athletic departments choose to run when one of their football players is reported to have committed sexual assault fall under a section in the playbook labeled, "Nothing to See Here."

Perhaps this is why so many victims feel that universities don't care about them, though they obviously care about football. Forgetting the ethical duties of universities to respond to reports of sexual assault, under Title IX, a federal law, they are legally mandated to care. If a school receives any federal money, it is obligated to protect every student's access to education, determined to be a civil right in this country. According to the advocacy group Know Your IX, "Schools must take immediate steps to address any sex discrimination, sexual harassment, or sexual violence on campus to prevent it from affecting students further. If a school knows or reasonably should know about discrimination, harassment, or violence that is creating a 'hostile environment' for any student, it must act to eliminate it, remedy the harm caused, and prevent its recurrence."[82]

The idea that universities don't care about victims is perceived to be worse whenever the accused is a high-profile athlete, someone the school has a serious financial and emotional stake in. In a July 2014 US Senate report titled, "Sexual Violence on Campus: How Too Many Institutions Are Failing to Protect Students," it was revealed that, "many institutions also use different adjudication procedures for student-athletes. More than 20 percent of institutions in the national sample give the athletic department oversight of sexual violence cases involving student-athletes. Approximately 20 percent of the nation's largest public institutions and 15 percent of the largest private institutions allow their athletic departments to oversee cases involving student-athletes."[83] This probably isn't surprising news to most people. A March 2015 HBO *Real Sports*/Marist Poll found that "nearly six in ten residents, 58 percent, think [athletes] are treated differently, including 36 percent who believe they are given greater slack and 22 percent who say they are held to a tougher standard."[84]

"The university knew and they just didn't care because they were playing good football," Kathy Redmond said in 2004 about how Nebraska responded in 1991 when she reported that player Christian Peter had raped her. (Peter, though later convicted of sexually assaulting another woman, still denies that he assaulted Redmond.) Redmond says that "she received death threats and prank phone calls (with the callers playing the Nebraska fight song). Her car was vandalized, and she says she was trailed by a private investigator."[85] Brown was the first person to ever file a lawsuit under Title IX about how the university mistreated her following her reporting that she had been assaulted; she settled with the school. Redmond went on to found National Coalition Against Violent Athletes; Peter went into the NFL and was later inducted into the Nebraska Football Hall of Fame.

To be sure, universities across the board have problems with how they handle sexual assault cases on their campus. That is why at the end of 2015, there were over 200 pending investigations at the Department of Education of universities that had possibly violated Title IX, all complaints filed by students. But there is a particular pattern (as there always seems to be) with cases involving athletes: for universities, it's about football first.

II.

Some of the most common plays in the "Nothing To See Here" section of the playbook:

A. The "Shhhhhh": A woman sued the University of Washington saying that after she reported being raped by a football player in 2001, "Instead of directing her to police, university officials suggested mediation—a confidential process in which she and [the accused] sat down together with the university's ombudswoman and a senior associate athletic director to discuss what had happened."[86]

B. The "Take Some Time Off": In 2003, when Florida State's vice president of Student Affairs intervened in Travis Johnson's case (discussed in Chapter 2), it was to get the woman to drop the charges in exchange for Johnson leaving campus for six months, in time to return for the next football season.

C. The "But He's Good": In 2009, the then-freshman kicker at Michigan was arrested for allegedly raping a freshman at fraternity house party.[87] She says she was then threatened by a different football player; no criminal charges were filed, and the accused kicked the game-winning field goal at the 2011 Sugar Bowl. The player was then expelled in January 2014 for what had happened back in 2009.

D. The "Hurry Up and Move On": In 2013, football players at Hobart and William Smith Colleges were never disciplined for allegedly sexually assaulting a student.[88] In fact, it only took the university twelve days to clear them, despite the woman saying there were multiple witnesses, including her friend who found her during the assault. The men's semen was found in her vagina, her rectum, and on her underwear. The team had an undefeated season.

E. The "Isolated Event": In 2015, after a string of players over a period of a few months had been accused of rape at Tennessee, head coach Butch Jones responded to the latest allegation by stating, "I don't want that to take away from all the great things that are going on in this football program . . . It's not an illustration of our football program."[89] It never is.

III.

Then there's a slightly more insidious play: the "Call the Cops." An alarming aspect of college football sexual assault cases is the underreported issue of the overlap between police and athletic departments.

Often, that overlap is innocuous. The *Chicago Tribune* reported in December 2014 on the city's athletic departments hiring off-duty cops to provide transportation escorts for their teams.[90] When they contacted the spokesman for Northwestern's football team to ask about the team paying for Illinois State Police for these escorts for them and any visiting team, he told the *Tribune*, "It is a courtesy reciprocated throughout college football. We take care of [the escort] in order to avoid the potential delays associated with transporting a large group through a densely populated area . . . on a tight timeline."

Coaches also use escorts on and off the field during games. When Pat Forde reported on this phenomenon for ESPN in 2006, he said, "It's mostly about status—for the coach and for the cops, who seem to excel at working their way into the background of TV shots."[91] Major Cary Sutton of the Alabama State Police, a sixteen-year veteran at the time, said cops enjoy the job because "it's kind of a little plum detail if you're a football fan." He also added that "every football-playing college—from Alabama to Alabama A&M—has a contract with the state police to provide support." Another cop who had worked with Troy's football team for a dozen years, Forde writes, "is so much a part of the program at Troy that when the Trojans made their first-ever bowl trip, to California for the Silicon Valley Bowl in 2004, he got a bowl ring." A sergeant with the West Virginia State Police told him that swag from teams "is one of the perks of being on the detail."

But the overlap is also not innocuous, which is the problem with there being any relationship at all. In June 2015, *Outside the Lines* reported that there is often confusion of boundaries between athletic departments and police, both local and campus.[92] "Athletic department officials inserted themselves into investigations many times. Some tried to control when and where police talked with athletes; others insisted on being present during player interviews, alerted defense attorneys, conducted their own investigations before contacting police, or even, in one case, handled potential crime-scene evidence." Part of the problem was that "some police officials were torn about proper procedure—unsure when to seek a coach's or athletic director's assistance when investigating crimes."

Barry Switzer, who left his successful career at Oklahoma in

1989 on the heels of his team being put on NCAA probation—players claiming drug use, and multiple players charged with first-degree rape—told *USA Today* in October 2014 that law enforcement were lax on his team.[93] "I'd have local county people call me and say, 'One of your guys is drunk and got in a fight and is in jail down here,'" Switzer said. "I'd go down and get him out. Or I'd send an assistant coach down to get his ass out. The sheriff was a friend of the program. He didn't want the publicity. He himself knew this was something we didn't need to deal with in the media or anything with publicity." He went on to say that was the norm at the time: "Most coaches ran it that way. We all did." In 2002, Kathy Redmond told ESPN, "There is such an incestuous relationship [between police and athletic departments] . . . It's very frightening."[94]

In August 2010, Lizzy Seeberg, a student at St. Mary's College just down the street from Notre Dame, reported to Notre Dame's police that a football player had sexually assaulted her. "He started sucking my neck and I started crying harder," Lizzy wrote in her statement to the campus police. "He pulled down my tank top by the straps. He slipped them down my shoulders and proceeded to suck and lick my right breast while holding me down on his lap by the arms. I felt his hands start to move down towards my shorts as if he was trying to unbutton them or pull them off. I was still crying at this point and felt so scared that I couldn't move." He did not rape her. No one interviewed the football player for fifteen days. Seeberg committed suicide in the meantime, after receiving threats from another player, according to Seeberg's friend, that read, "Don't do anything you would regret," and, "Messing with Notre Dame football is a bad idea." That second text, said her father, who visited her the weekend after she filed the report, bothered her more than anything." A retired Notre Dame police officer, Pat Cottrell told

a reporter that "the university effectively makes it more difficult to investigate student-athletes by barring police from going
through the athletic department."[95] In the documentary *The
Hunting Ground*, Cottrell says of his former employer, "There
was a directive that the campus police cannot contact an athlete at any athletic facility, and we cannot contact any athletic
employee to assist us in contacting the athlete that we would be
looking for." When asked why this is a rule, Cottrell responds
simply, "I guess just to keep us away from student-athletes." The
football player is now in the NFL. In May 2015, he was charged
with killing his former girlfriend's dog. This is no small point,
the killing of the dog: "Seventy-one percent of pet-owning
women entering women's shelters reported that their batterer
had injured, maimed, killed, or threatened family pets for
revenge or to psychologically control victims."[96]

In October 2014, Mike McIntire and Walt Bogdanich were
clear about how incestuous this was at FSU, showing how the
Tallahassee police officers' bank accounts profited from the program: "A successful football program is also good for Tallahassee
police officers. They earn an extra $40 to $45 an hour, at university expense, providing traffic control on game days, according to the department. Last season, officers were paid a total of
$112,000, according to the university."[97] Also, when TPD got
the records request from a sport reporter out of Tampa, the *New
York Times* found that e-mails were sent between the TPD and
the campus police chief, and then between the campus police
chief and the FSU athletic department regarding the reporter,
asking if they could legally stop his request.

It's a good move to call the cops when you think they will
help you execute your "Nothing to See Here" play, especially
if the cop you are calling is wearing a bowl game ring on his
finger. University and athletic officials should have to answer

hard questions about what these overlaps mean for determining guilt, dispensing justice, and protecting all students' civil rights.

IV.

There's the straight-up "Interference" move. The most famous case of interference is Montana's Robin Pflugrad, who was head coach there for two seasons, from 2010 to 2012.

In 2010, a woman reported to the Missoula police that multiple football players had raped her at a party. The police were not kind to her. According to the local paper, the *Missoulian*, "The US Department of Justice would later find flaws in MPD's handling of [the woman's] case and several others. The report, released in May 2013, would criticize MPD for interviewing sexual assault victims in a way 'more appropriate for an interrogation of a suspect than a crime victim.'"[98] They found the police slow to act, giving the players time to get their stories together, and that the cops failed to understand the relationship between alcohol and consent. Charges were never pressed, something the Missoula County Attorney told CBS's *60 Minutes* was an easy decision. That same *60 Minutes* episode in 2014 suggested that Pflugrad knew the woman had reported but never informed school officials.

In his recent book, *Missoula*[99], Jon Krakauer investigates a series of reported sexual assaults in Missoula between 2010 and 2012—some, like the one above, involving Montana football players. He reports that the quarterback, Jordan Johnson, received notification from a dean that the administrator had "found sufficient evidence that you violated the Student Conduct Code" by raping a fellow student in February 2012 and that the dean would "seek your immediate explusion from the university." The QB went to Robin Pflugrad's home and pleaded his innocence to the coach, who, Krakauer writes, "assured his nineteen-year-old quarterback that everything 'was going to be okay.'" Pflugrad then called the athletic director immediately and, Krakauer says, "the UM athletic department promptly mobilized to do everything possible to defend Johnson against" the allegations.

Johnson was briefly suspended from the team, but when the restraining order against him was replaced with a "no-contact order," Pflugrad, the Associated Press reports, "welcomed Johnson back, and touted the 'character and tremendous moral fiber' of the player he had known since Johnson was a boy."[100] Pflugrad's contract with Montana was not renewed three days later. Johnson was later charged with felony sexual intercourse without consent, kicked off the team, expelled, tried, found not guilty, returned to Montana and the team, and was playing in the CFL until he was cut from Ottawa in May 2015. Johnson sued Montana and in February 2016 settled with them in exchange for him dropping his claims. As part of the settlement, no one had to admit liability regarding Johnson's expulsion.

The Montana football team won their conference championship in 2011 and Pflugrad won coach of the year for the conference. When his contract was not renewed, the university president did not explain his decision. Pflugrad went on to be offensive coordinator at Weber State. He was punished by the NCAA in 2013 for his time at Montana, not with regard to the sexual assault allegations but rather for not monitoring his program sufficiently and allowing boosters to financially compensate two players by providing bail and legal counsel to them. (They were arrested while police were breaking up a party.) He missed the first game of Weber State's 2013 season and his ability to recruit was temporarily restricted. He apparently hasn't coached since the end of that season.

In July 2013, Pflugrad told the AP that "the administration overreacted" at Montana when it fired him.[101]

V.

The "Repeat Offender." Coaches like second chances. They often give them to their players alongside a reasonable helping of assuming the best in their players. After all, sports are supposed to craft boys into men, to make them responsible sportsmen with impeccable character, molded by the coaches who oversee their development.

The problem occurs when the second chance simply leaves space for a player to do the same bad behavior all over again. It is only the player, though, who faces the consequences for his repeated behavior, never the men around him who enabled him by looking away, by hiding under the redemptive language of "second chances," by always seeming to imagine that their player didn't do that bad thing.

Perhaps the most shocking version of the "Repeat Offender" happened in 2004. The summer of 2003, Dirk Koetter, the head coach at Arizona State, intervened when an incoming football player was expelled from what ESPN described as "a four-week transition program designed to help incoming freshmen adjust to college life." The player had been kicked out for "grabbing and touching women in the dorm, exposing himself to female staff members, and threatening freshman women." According to ESPN, he had also "told an ASU official that he wanted women to fear him and that it was important for him to 'show them their place.'"[102] But Koetter convinced officials to let the player return to campus that fall. The following spring, a woman reported that the player stalked and then raped her. ASU police tried to interview the player but it took three weeks, and when they did get to talk to him, the director of football operations was at his side. After catching the player in lies, the police pushed the case to the county DA who decided not to press charges. Then, ESPN says, after the player was expelled, "Koetter tried to help him obtain a scholarship at Arkansas–Pine Bluff and other programs." In 2009, the woman settled with ASU, getting a large sum of money, along with the demand that ASU create a "highly placed safety officer who will review and reform policies for reporting and investigating incidents of sexual harassment and assault."

Koetter's choice to ignore his players' abusive behavior toward women turned absolutely tragic in 2005. That March, Loren Wade, a star running back for ASU, shot and killed Brandon Falkner, a former player, after, some witnesses say, Wade told Falkner, "You ain't talking to my girl."[103] According to a 2007 article at the *Phoenix New Times*, Wade was suspended in 2004 "after accepting payments from an athletic department friend with whom he'd had a sexual affair."[104] Koetter let him back on the team in 2005, despite the fact that he "was aware that Wade had threatened to kill a female gymnast. Koetter also had received a report from ASU's women's soccer coach that players were terrified because Wade possessed a gun. He also knew that Wade's girlfriend had called police, fearing Wade was going to destroy her apartment after he threatened her life." Koetter, the *Phoenix New Times* says, did not report any of that to the university but instead "elected to counsel Wade personally." Wade's attorney told the paper that the coaching staff "sort of just let it go on." The school acknowledged in July 2005 that Koetter did not make good choices regarding Wade, but in December 2005 he got a contract extension through 2009 and a raise that put his paycheck near $1 million a year.

When Koetter suspended Wade in fall 2004—which must have happened within months, if not weeks after Koetter begged the school to let back in the player who would go on to rape another ASU student—Koetter filled Wade's position with another player who had his own history of sexual assault allegations. In 2000, according to ESPN, Hakim Hill, while still in high school, was "charged with third-degree sexual assault after being accused of locking himself in a City High classroom with a fifteen-year-old girl and forcing her to have sex. He escaped jail time by entering an Alford plea, meaning he did not admit guilt but acknowledged that prosecutors had enough evidence to convict him at trial."[105] By December 2004, Hill was off the team too. He had violated team rules by punching a teammate before their bowl game that year. Koetter announced Hill's dismissal by saying, "We always give players second chances, because college is a growing and learning process. But there are certain lines that can't be crossed, and when they are, you have to take the appropriate action."[106] Hill transferred immediately to Northern Iowa, a Division I Football Championship Subdivision program, and played ball for them.

Koetter didn't make it through 2006 before he was fired—because he wasn't winning football games, not because of the violence his players were committing off the field. He eventually ended up working with the Tampa Bay Buccaneers as their offensive coordinator and his quarterback was rookie Jameis Winston. When the Bucs fired their head coach after the end of the regular 2015 season, Koetter took over that position.

One can understand why Dirk Koetter likes the idea of second chances, seeing as he has benefited from them repeatedly.

VI.

Sometimes, there's just the good old "Pretend Everything Is Fine" play. Missouri is a great example of this and how it can be implemented over and over again for years, if necessary.

Columbia, Missouri, home to the university, sits in the center of the state, with Kansas City to the west and St. Louis to the east.[107] Its population of roughly 115,000 people is sometimes called "The Athens of Missouri," "in reference to the politically liberal–leaning students who . . . have significant influence over the town."

The university, which has roughly 35,000 students, is home to the only Division I-A athletics program in the state. According to *US News & World Report*, "The Missouri Tigers teams are a big focus of campus life. The teams compete in the NCAA Division I Southeastern Conference and are particularly competitive in football." In 2013, the year Missouri's Michael Sam won co–defensive player in the SEC, they went 13–2, 7–1 in the SEC, playing in the SEC title game against Auburn. They went on to beat Oklahoma State at the Cotton Bowl.

The success of the sports program under the tenure of Mike Alden, who was the athletic director there from 1998 until 2015, is indisputable and was thusly lauded on his Missouri bio page while he was there: "Since beginning his seventeen-year stint in Columbia, however, Alden has seen several programs rise to the level of national championship contenders, highlighted by conference championships in football, men's basketball, volleyball, soccer, softball, baseball, and wrestling, including three league titles last season alone." He raised a substantial amount of money to renovate the football stadium, which the site assured us "will make the home of Tiger Football one of the finest in America."

What Alden's bio failed to mention was that he had also overseen a series of failures when it came to how his department handled off-field issues with players, specifically incidents involving basketball and football and violence against women.

In 2014, ESPN's *Outside the Lines* issued major reports about two different sexual assault allegations.[108] The first, published in January, was about a possible gang rape in February

2010 by football players of a fellow student-athlete, Sasha Menu Courey, who later committed suicide. The report alleges that in May 2011, a few months before she died, Menu Courey told an athletic staffer about the assault, but despite a federal legal obligation under Title IX for that staffer to alert the university, an investigation was never conducted. Chad Moller, the athletic department spokesman, told ESPN, "The university, in declining to launch an investigation, is honoring what it believes were the wishes of Menu Courey, who never reported the incident to police."

Then, in late August, the second *Outside the Lines* report drew more scrutiny on the team and the athletic department. Running back Derrick Washington, who left the school in 2010 after he was arrested and charged with sexual assault, had at least two other violent incidents with women before that assault and another before he left the team. (He disputes the allegations unearthed by *Outside the Lines*.) In October 2008, a fellow student reported that Washington assaulted her in her dorm room. She went to campus police, who after an investigation found probable cause to issue a warrant for his arrest on a charge of forcible rape. The county DA refused that warrant, stating, "There are too many inconsistencies in the victim's story to ensure a reasonable probability that a jury would convict on a charge of forcible rape." Instead, the DA "contacted the defense attorney and entered into an agreement whereby the defendant [Washington] agrees to have no contact with the victim and complete rape awareness classes within a year."

In May 2010, a month before Washington committed the sexual assault for which he was convicted, a female Missouri soccer player reported that he had punched her in the face while she was fighting with Washington's girlfriend at a bar. The player reported it to the police "and a warrant was issued for third-degree assault. But later that day, she came to the police department and said she had changed her mind." Her backtrack, she said, was because "she believed her scholarship was in danger, because of her arrest . . . her coach pointed out that if Mr. Washington was arrested the incident would make the news and the situation with her scholarship might change." ESPN reported that "she did lose her scholarship but, with the help of an attorney, was able to have it reinstated." The chancellor of Missouri says the claim to revoke the player's scholarship based on her pressing charges is "unsubstantiated." Instead, the school officially says that they "did send her a letter dated June 29, 2010, informing her that she was going to lose her scholarship. [The university spokesman] said that letter was sent inadvertently." It's worth nothing that Menu Courey, two weeks after she supposedly told the athletic staffer that she had been raped by a football player, received a letter saying she was no longer eligible for financial aid. According to ESPN, "Missouri officials told 'Outside the Lines' the letter was a form letter sent to 1,472 students, and it was not referring to her athletic scholarship."

In June, Washington sexually assaulted another woman in her apartment. He was charged with felony deviant sexual assault in late August. Within two weeks of being charged, he was arrested again, this time for domestic assault in the third degree against his girlfriend. He would be convicted a year later for the sexual assault. According to ESPN, "A judge sentenced him to five years in prison. He served four months as part of a first-time offenders program and had to register as a sex offender." Then, in February 2012, he pleaded guilty to the domestic assault charge, and served ninety days for it concurrently with the sexual assault sentence.

Washington's 2008 sexual assault was also mishandled. In fact, head football coach Gary Pinkel knew of the incident, but never disciplined Washington; Athletic Director Mike Alden never called for an investigation. In August 2014, Pinkel and Alden held a joint press conference immediately following the release of the second *Outside the Lines* report in which they explained these actions. Pinkel said, "If [the police] don't charge him, how am I supposed to, unless there's other circumstances or things I know." Alden, for his part, said he was ignorant of Title IX regulations: "But back in 2008, I was not aware of those types of procedures and how they took place on campus."

Pinkel also told the press that when the 2010 allegations came to light, he spoke to Washington and "I just told Mike that there's no way in the world, knowing he very likely is gonna get arrested in the middle of September, can we play the first game with him. We can't do it. I had enough information that we would make that decision. And that's what we did. We suspended him prior to [the season]." Yet, in 2013, Jeff Benedict and Armen Keteyian, in their book *The System: The Glory and Scandal of Big-Time College Football*, write that Washington's mother said, "Coach Pinkel called and told us he was permanently suspended. He said he fought for Derrick for over an hour. But he said the curators, essentially the school's trustees, called him in and told him what they were going to do. He said he wanted to redshirt Derrick until after the trial. And if the trial went well, he'd reinstate him and play him the following year. But the curators wouldn't go for that."[109] (The Board of Curators is the governing body of the University of Missouri.) It's clear when reading *The System* that Benedict and Keteyian wrote about the 2010 sexual assault case against Washington without knowing about the 2008 one.

Yet, there's more to this than what appears in the *Outside the Lines* reports. In 2010, when the campus detective arrived at the victim's apartment to look into the second Washington allegation, he already knew the victim's roommate. In January of that year, she had called the campus police when, she said, she had been sexually assaulted by a Missouri basketball player. This was a month before Sasha Menu Courey said she had been assaulted by multiple Missouri football players. According to *The System*, the roommate "underwent a rape kit at the hospital, and [the detective] conducted the criminal investigation. In his report, he noted that 'she was afraid of what might happen' if she pressed charges. Ultimately, [she] declined to cooperate with prosecutors, choosing instead to meet with the head basketball coach, which led to [the player] issuing her an apology. She dropped her complaint at that point." That basketball player? He left Missouri in November 2012 after a second rape allegation (which also didn't lead to charges).

Alden's tenure at Missouri was a troubled one when it comes to the behavior of players off the field, especially violence against women. Louis Moore, associate professor of history at Grand Valley State University, told me that "Missouri has an ugly history under AD Mike Alden of guys given multiple chances after nasty charges. In 2003, for example, the school allowed basketball point guard Ricky Clemons to remain in school [he was suspended for a year] and participate in team functions after he pleaded guilty to false imprisonment and third-degree assault." Clemons had "pushed [a woman] down, bloodied her nose, and choked her after she refused to watch the movie *Roots* with him." Moore also brought up Alvin Newhouse, a linebacker for Missouri who was charged with forcible rape, sodomy, and attempted forcible rape in 2004.[110] Newhouse, unlike Clemons, was dismissed from the team once charges were filed. He would later plead guilty to sexual misconduct, a misdemeanor.

In spring of 2014, seven Missouri athletes were arrested within a three-month period. According to a *Kansas City Star* report released in June 2014, those arrests included multiple football and basketball players being arrested for drug possession, as well as Zach Price, a basketball player, and Dorian Green-Beckham, a football player, each being arrested within days of one another in early April for domestic assault. The latter two were dismissed from their teams. Green-Beckham was never charged.

In June 2015, *OTL* reported that Green-Beckham's girlfriend at the time texted the woman who had reported him and wrote, "He will be kicked out of Mizzou and then not qualify for the [NFL] draft next year. The coaches talked to me and explained how serious this is and there's no time to waste at this point." When the police asked to clarify what exactly the coaches had said to her and if they asked her to try to get the charges dropped, ESPN reports, "she changed her story and said the coaches never talked to her directly but that Green-Beckham had told her to relay the information." Whatever the story, it worked. The woman dropped charges and was explicit about why she did it: "She stated she was afraid of the media and community backlash since Green-Beckham is a football player. [She] was afraid of being harassed and having her property damaged just because she was the victim. [She] stated she did not want to deal with the mental stress of the whole ordeal; it was already making her physically sick to think about it."

At a press conference Pinkel and Alden held in response to the August 2014 *OTL* report, Pinkel said that he dismissed Green-Beckham without charges because "I had other information, quite honestly, that I knew that would help me make a decision, and the decision was that I had to remove him. It's confidential where I got that and how I got that. I could have thrown it out, but I didn't, because I have to do what's right."

This then raises questions about the 2008 allegation against Washington: Did Coach Pinkel know that Washington had to take rape awareness classes mandated by the county DA? Did Washington take them? Did the coach know he took them? Why were charges the threshold for determining whether to discipline a player and whether the player had to take rape awareness classes mandated by the county DA?

In September 2014, I asked Chad Moller, the spokesman for the Missouri athletic department, these exact questions. I also asked him if Washington's mother's account given to Benedict and Keteyian about Pinkel advocating for Washington to remain on the team in 2010 even if charged with sexual assault was true. I also inquired about the current protocol for determining at what point the team suspends a player once sexual allegations have been made. Moller told me, "We've addressed these issues, which happened more than six years ago, and we're focused on learning from the experience and improving our procedures and moving forward. Along those lines, I've attached a statement from Chancellor Dr. R. Bowen Loftin that you're welcome to use. Hope this is helpful." When I wrote him back and asked, "So, fair to say you are no longer answering specific questions about 2008 or 2010 then?" I never received a response.

As for what the football team is specifically doing to help prevent sexual assault by players in the future, Pinkel told reporters that Cornell Ford, the cornerbacks coach, "handles that every year in August with our team, he's very specific about rape and no is no, and so on and so forth." In a follow-up to these comments, the *Missourian* interviewed players about what Ford does to address sexual assault: "[Mitch] Morse [a team captain and senior offensive tackle] remembered Ford talking with the team about respecting women and sexual assault for five minutes at one point during two-a-day practices. Darius White, a senior wide receiver, remembered a ten- to twelve-minute conversation after practice."[111] There is nothing specific in Ford's background that explains why he is the coach on staff who handles these discussions.

This matters because part of what *Outside the Lines* uncovered in the 2008 case against Washington was a video of the detective interviewing Washington about what had happened that night. We see Washington sitting across a small table from the detective in a room. "What exactly does she say?" the detective asks Washington. "Just that she doesn't want to have sex," he replies. The detective then asks if he can remember how many times she said that she didn't want to have sex. Washington: "Maybe three." The detective then asks him, "How long was your penis inside of her before she said stop?" Washington says, "About thirty seconds maybe and then she said stop, and then I stopped. Then she started crying." The detective then asks if the victim physically fought back by pushing on Washington's chest. "Fuck no," Washington quickly answers. Finally, the detective asks, "Do you acknowledge that what happened shouldn't have happened?" Washington immediately says, "Yeah. It shouldn't have happened. It shouldn't have happened." The detective follows up with, "Do you acknowledge that what happened could be possibly considered to be an assault of some sort?" Washington: "No."

While Morse told the *Missourian* that "treating women with respect" is one of the "core values" of the Missouri football team, that does not mean that they are teaching them exactly what constitutes sexual assault and, more importantly, what consent looks like. After everything we now know about how little Alden and Pinkel did in the face of serious allegations against a player (and the resulting effect of that same player going on to harm multiple other women), why we should be satisfied with a coach teaching the team "so on and so forth" about sexual assault is puzzling.

Alden retired in early 2015. He moved into Missouri's College of Education where he is an instructor in the Positive Coaching Program. Gary Pinkel announced that 2015–16 season would be his last, as he was diagnosed earlier that year with lymphoma. Both men were praised for their work, though most discussions of their legacies mention how they did not respond well to violent off-field behavior by their athletes.

VII.

"It's Not Us But Them." In January 2016, Erica Kinsman settled her Title IX suit with FSU. (She had a second suit against Winston himself.) The university agreed to pay her $950,000, to set up a five-year plan to address awareness, prevention, and training around sexual assault on campus, and to not admit liability. The university president, John Thrasher, released a statement in which he wrote that "we regret we will never be able to tell our full story in court."[112] He explained that the decision to settle came about because it would cost too much to see the case through, and added, "With all the economic demands we face, at some point it doesn't make sense to continue even though we are convinced we would have prevailed." He also noted pointedly, "Kinsman is expected to receive $250,000 while her attorneys will get more than twice that amount—$700,000." Kinsman's attorney's immediately disputed his breakdown of her part of the settlement. For Thrasher, though, this is not about what FSU did or did not do when a survivor reported that an athlete had raped her, it's about her greedy lawyers and their big pockets. It is never us, it is always them.

Of course, there were things left out of Thrasher's statement. As Joe Nocera at the *New York Times* writes, "He failed to note that Winston's scheduled deposition was only three weeks away, and that those who were to give depositions also included two other football players; an associate athletic director, Monk Bonasorte, who appears to be the team's fixer; and the campus police chief."[113]

Also, there's the fact that of the $1.7 million in legal fees that FSU owed, the vast majority, $1.3 million, were paid by the athletic department's booster club. This can be taken two ways. The charitable reading is that FSU wanted to punish athletics and so made them pay for this case. FSU administration is saying, "It's not us, it's the athletics department and they will take responsibility." The cynical reading is that for the booster club, this amount is, as Kavitha A. Davidson at *Bloomberg View* writes, "a drop in the bucket compared to the $7.6 million in program revenue and $35.5 million in total revenue the boosters raised during the 2013–14 fiscal year."[114] Maybe the boosters got off easy and this is not punishment but rather a club that shows it is willing to pay to keep problematic players on the field and their cases under the rug. Davidson adds that this makes sense within the larger system, where the NCAA has "penalized [schools] for boosters providing free legal advice to players, yet here we have boosters covering the services of legal counsel to the university."

For Nocera, this settlement is indicative of an entire university that failed Kinsman. "Everything Florida State has done since the beginning of the Winston affair," Nocera writes, "from looking the other way until a national championship was in hand, to using the settlement to heap scorn on the accuser's lawsuit—has sent one message to its student: Athletic achievement matters more than students' safety." Indeed, all of it casts serious doubt over Thrasher's statement that FSU "remains committed to making our campus safe for all students and our school free of sexual harassment and sexual assault."

What survivor watching not only how FSU handled Kinsman's case after she reported but how they continued to demean her in the press as she sought to hold them accountable for their failures would feel safe reporting to that administration? When Thrasher creates a narrative that it is others who have wronged FSU, not that FSU has wronged, does he not care that survivors might identify much more strongly with the "others" than with FSU?

VIII.

There are too many reasons for universities to minimize and even ignore reports of sexual violence done by their football players. These players are the cogs in their lucrative machines and must be protected. A reminder: these are mainly white men—university presidents, athletic directors, coaches. Their faces and names are too rarely centered when we discuss this problem. But they are making decisions that prioritize the success of their teams over and above the safety of other students and the community at large. And they have so many ways to do it. Don't be fooled the next time a case breaks and the university and athletic officials throw out a "Nothing to See Here" play from the playbook. It's what they know; it's what they do.

The Shrug

I.

While universities attempt to pull the wool over people's eyes, the NCAA has perfected the part of the playbook known as "The Shrug." When asked by the *Huffington Post* in early 2015 how the NCAA, with its near-billion-dollar annual revenue, remains a nonprofit, they said, "As a nonprofit organization, we put our money where our mission is: equipping student-athletes to succeed on the playing field, in the classroom, and throughout life."[115] But when athletes are committing violence off the field and some of the most high-profile victims and survivors of sexual assault by college football players are former student-athletes, one has to seriously question what the NCAA means. It is never the NCAA's job to do anything about the problem of sexual violence committed by student-athletes—so says the NCAA.

So, why does the NCAA exist? According to its website, the 110-year-old institution exists so its "more than 1,200 schools, conferences, and affiliate organizations" can "collectively invest in improving the experiences of student-athletes—on the field, in the classroom, and in life." It most often makes the news when it is levying fines and punishments against big-time coaches and programs for violations of their regulations, or fighting in court to continue not paying athletes but to still make money off their names and images. And it's a really cozy setup for everyone involved. The rules that govern the participants in the NCAA are set by the participants: commissioners of conferences, university presidents, and athletic directors sit on committees that agree upon what behaviors will be regulated. In short, it's big, it's old, it's rich, it's white, it's male, it's powerful, and we've reached a point where it seems impossible to imagine any other system. It is the devil we all know.

But it's still a devil. It's hard to find anyone outside of the NCAA who likes the NCAA. So many programs spend a lot of their time trying to best the devil, to skirt its rules, and to take advantage of the lax enforcement. And when it comes to the problem of sexual violence, while universities and their athletic departments act like it is no big deal, the devil's response is often to act like this simply isn't its problem to deal with.

II.

The NCAA's most basic move: "Ignore it." In the big business of college football, if athletic directors and coaches want to keep their high-powered and high-profile jobs, they have to win. To do that, they need the best players on the field. (Drafting and calling plays only gets you so far if you don't have the best athletes to execute them.) Convincing the best football players to attend your school and play for you is imperative. Per NCAA regulations, which I'll reiterate are set by administrators and athletic officials from the universities and conferences, athletic departments are extremely limited in what they can offer to recruits.

The NCAA Division I manual is over four hundred pages long. The section on recruitment stretches fifty-nine pages. If you've never had the pleasure of reading those fifty-nine pages, what is allowed and what is prohibited is laid out in painstaking detail. For example, "An institution may not provide a prospective student-athlete with transportation to attend an off-campus contest outside a thirty-mile radius of the member institution's main campus." The rules dictate what video and audio materials an institution may provide to a recruit, when exactly a forty-eight-hour official visit begins and ends (it "begins at the time the prospective student-athlete arrives on the institution's campus, rather than with the initiation of the prospective student-athlete's transportation by a coach or the time of the prospective student-athlete's arrival at the airport or elsewhere in the community," in case you were wondering), and there are four pages that outline who can call a prospective athlete and for how long.

Most famously, the NCAA bans teams from offering any financial incentives above and beyond the promise of a set scholarship amount. This is what gains most of the attention in the news. The NCAA is very interested in maintaining the supposed amateurism of college sports. To do so, it monitors if boosters (financial supporters of a university or team) provide recruits or players with any kind of compensation and if players have made any money off their own image, jersey, or signature. The NCAA will smoke that out and fine schools, take away wins, and prohibit teams from participating in the postseason. And it is always news.

What isn't found in those fifty-nine pages on recruitment is what would be perhaps the most basic rule the NCAA could lay down if it wants us to believe it is serious about the problem of sexual violence: don't use women and/or sex to sell your school to incoming athletes. Are you the head of a high-powered college football team and you want to use women in recruitment? Okay, go ahead.

And it's not like the NCAA doesn't know about this problem.

The NCAA simply, it seems, doesn't ever want to talk about it.

Along with the promise of great coaching, top-notch facilities, a path to the pros, and the possibility of being on TV, schools use the official forty-eight-hour campus visits that top recruits make to their favorite schools to show these high school boys what their everyday experience on campus would be like if they choose to attend that university. Starting with legendary Alabama football coach Bear Bryant in the 1960s, large Division I athletic programs at major universities have been using groups called "hostesses"—college women with pretty, smiling faces who assist high-caliber potential student-athletes when they visit campus—as an important part of recruitment visits.

Thirty years ago, these groups were celebrated in weirdly sexist fashion in the pages of *Sports Illustrated*. In 1987, *SI* ran a piece by Alexander Wolff titled "The Fall Roundup: Persuasive Hostesses Help College Lasso Top Prospects" in their college football preview issue.[116] In the piece, Betty Ling, the woman in charge of the all-female recruitment squad for the University of Florida, the Gator Getters, sounds like a matchmaker on a reality TV dating show. Her job was to pick the perfect hostess from a sea of beautiful women ("They come in all shapes and sizes," the piece quotes Ling. "We got tall ones, short ones, and wide ones. Hopefully, no obese ones.") and pair that hostess up with a potential recruit. "A Gator Getter can be the most fetching woman on campus, but she's of no use to Betty if she can't translate that fetching into some fetch," Wolff writes. "'We don't have posters or calendars of the girls,' she says. 'We're not trying to sell the Gator Getters. We're selling the University of Florida. Recruits fall in love with 'em, sure. But that's not why they end up coming here.'" Ling later says that the name is suggestive and they'd thought about changing it but, since it's tradition, they had left it alone. The woman in charge of Auburn's recruitment tells Wolff, "If groups nationwide are anything like ours they deserve a lot of credit. Our coaches say these girls are the heartbeat of recruiting."

Wolff implies heavily that the women are selling the idea of sex to these high school boys (though also hints that they don't actually have sex with the recruits): "The savvy hostess uses allure as a lure, up to a point. Tracey Ryan, a Washington State hostess, is not available. 'But,' she says, 'it's not like you want them to know that. Let them come to school here and find out.'" And even when Wolff mentions male hosts, he makes sure to tell us, "He'll likely introduce you to a wide cross-section of young women, including those who won't necessarily be bound to the hostesses' code of conduct."

Ashley Witherspoon, who was shot and raped by a former FSU football player in December 1993, told *Deadspin*: "When I was at Florida State there were these 'Bat Girls'—maybe they're still there—and they were used for recruiting purposes for the baseball team. Why do high school seniors and college freshmen need beautiful girls to show them around and take them out? What's really going on? What are we teaching them? What are we offering them? I'm not making excuses for offenders, but sex, drugs, and rock and roll is a big part of it."[117]

In 2002, the *Sun-Sentinel* ran a piece about football recruitment titled "Pretty Faces Make Good Recruiters" that included the following quote from a former UF receiver: "I think most people want to meet as many girls as they can. I think that's what attracts a lot of them to a program."[118]

That same year, HBO's *Real Sports* aired a piece in which two former hostesses from Oregon and a former member of the football team said that sex was part of recruitment for the football program. According to the local Eugene paper, the *Register-Guard*, a football player was quoted as saying one of the attractions for recruits on official forty-eight-hour visits to the university was "girls. Girls, girls, girls."[119] They also wrote that one of the women interviewed told *Real Sports* "that when hosting recruits, the women sometimes feel as though recruits 'expect you're going to do more than just be their guide.'" The *Register-Guard* piece also had a quote from another Oregon player, who said, "Girls and sex are part of a lot of people's trips. A lot of recruits base their judgment of how good a school was or how good that trip was on whether or not they got to meet a couple of young girls or hang out with a couple girls. It's definitely important to young kids." He did add, though, that the women who have sex with recruits at off-campus parties aren't necessarily hostesses.

It's worth noting that in May 2001, the year before this report came out, a junior at Oregon who worked in the equipment room said that a football player had raped her. She told her boss, who encouraged her to contact the head coach of the team, which she did. She quit her job so she wouldn't be near the player, found out she was pregnant, had an abortion, and then reported the rape to university officials that summer. Then, in November, frustrated by the fact that nothing was happening, she reported to the Eugene police. By that point, the player had hired an attorney. In December, the DA decided there was not enough evidence to take the case to court. Her case was not reported in the media until 2014 when she came forward after a woman reported that three Oregon basketball players had raped her.[120] (Charges were never filed in the 2014 case but the woman won in civil court against UO.)

In early 2003, the *State Press*, Arizona State's student newspaper, interviewed two female hostesses about what happened there during recruitment for football players.[121] According to the paper, the two women "don't condone or participate in what many of their peers are doing 'unofficially' as recruiters," but they did admit that "underage drinking and consensual sex between recruits and female recruiters are common." The head coach at the time, Dirk Koetter, told the paper, "It is a valuable part of recruiting student-athletes because the incoming student-athlete . . . they get to talk to some people who aren't just football players. They can offer some insight into student life that I certainly can't and the players can't." He went on: "The coaches that are running the Sun Devil Recruiters, I trust them and I know that they're doing the right things." This is the same man who, in the summer of 2004, intervened on behalf of a freshman football player who had been thrown out of school for sexually harassing and threatening women. The football player then stalked, harassed, and raped a student (see Chapter 3).

The Gator Getters were still around almost two decades after that *SI* feature on hostesses, though they had changed their named to the Gator Guides in the 1990s because, according to Betty Ling in a 2004 *Gainesville Sun* article, "Some groups got together and felt it could be considered too suggestive."[122] It's interesting that what was considered offensive and what changed was the name—perhaps the most superficial part of the group—not what they represented or symbolized to the recruits. The 2004 article says that the name change was important because "the old name—Gator Getters—implied the Gators might be using attractive females to help lure top recruits to Florida, which UF officials say wasn't true then and isn't true now." The line in 2004 was that while the women played an important role in recruitment, it was "limited." Ling: "Everything they [Gator Guides] do is in front of the coaching staff. We're very strict with our girls. We primarily use our players as hosts to the recruits and that's who they spend the most time with.

The Gator Guides are there to assist and answer questions about the university. We're not trying to sell the girls, we're trying to sell the University of Florida's academics. We have enough reasons to become a Gator than just because there's a pretty girl around." Much of the article consists of former Guides and players explaining how little contact the two groups had during recruitment, how strict then-coach Steve Spurrier was about that, and how it was never one-on-one contact. One former Gator Guide vociferously denies that they did anything beyond provide help for recruits; but "she knew of one incident that year where a Gator Guide and a recruit became romantically involved during a weekend visit. The player signed with Florida and is still on the team."

The point of using women in recruitment is not necessarily about providing recruits actual sex during recruitment (though certainly that happens). It's more about selling the idea that attending that particular university comes with the side benefit of being surrounded by pretty, accommodating women who are there to help you and care for you. In 2003, the assistant athletic director at Notre Dame, Mike Karowski, told Arizona State's *State Press*, "We've decided not to have a bunch of women hosting football players. There's no need. In fact, there's no need to have one of these programs anywhere. We're not selling sex here, and when you present a group of attractive females to a high school football player, that's the impression you're giving them."[123]

And it's an impression that has potentially dangerous side effects: the promise of women and sex as part of the Big Man on Campus player package. On its face there's nothing wrong with students showing around prospective students. The problem comes when programs run by older white men use female hosts specifically because they are women—and because their presence promises teenage boys and young men something more than a tour of the quad.

III.

On December 7, 2001, three women reported that football players and recruits from the University of Colorado had raped them, two at an off-campus party, the third in a dorm room.[124] The team had won the Big 12 championship the weekend before and was hosting recruits that weekend. In October 2003, District Attorney Mary Keenan gave a deposition in a lawsuit filed by one of the women. In that deposition she said that none of the players were charged because they believed they were attending a party where everyone there had already agreed to have consensual sex. "The recruits had third-party consent that had nothing to do with" the women, Keenan said. "They had been built up by the players to believe that the situation they were going into was specifically to provide them with sex. Their mind-set coming into it was that it was consensual because they had been told it had been set up for that very purpose, and that's what was going to happen." There is no legal concept of "third-party consent." Someone else cannot decide for you if something is consensual; that is actually the *opposite* of consent.

Colorado was not even new to these kinds of allegations. In 1997, four years earlier, a seventeen-year-old high school student reported that she went to a party for recruits, drank a lot, passed out, and woke up to a recruit raping her. He said it was consensual; she says it was not and that is why she ran down the hallway naked, screaming. She spoke to the *New York Times* in 2002, saying, "I feel strongly the entire party was a setup. I was invited there for the purpose of having sex with recruits, whether I was willing to or not, whether I consented or not."[125]

Keenan mirrored these thoughts in her October 2003 deposition. She said she believed the parties held during football recruitment were part of "an understanding that rose up in the culture" of the athletics department. She went so far as to call them "an expectation." Keenan also said that a former athletics official told her that the athletics department decided "they would not change anything because they could not afford to lose the competitive edge against universities such as Oklahoma [and] Nebraska." A campus police officer was deposed in May 2003, where he testified that he spoke to a recruit who said: "They told us, you know, 'This is what you get when you come to Colorado.'"

The coach at the time, Gary Barnett, responded to the allegations in the lawsuit by saying, "Neither Gary Barnett nor any coach has ever encouraged or condoned sex as a tool or part of the recruiting process, period. The accusation is wrong, inaccurate, false." By December 2005, Barnett was out of a job, which ESPN explained at the time this way: "On Thursday, [Barnett] reluctantly accepted a $3 million settlement, bringing to an end a tenure that was riddled by off-the-field problems but ultimately done in by recent bad results on the field."[126]

The off-the-field issues were significant, though. In February 2004, another woman came forward saying she had been raped four years earlier by a football player at Colorado. Katie Hnida was also a kicker on the team in 2000 when she says she was assaulted.[127] Additionally, Hnida talked of a program where she was verbally harassed and threatened. When asked about Hnida, Barnett spoke not of the allegations but instead her playing ability: "I think she was a distraction, because at the end of practice we would have twenty media members there to talk to a walk-on kicker who couldn't kick it through the uprights. That was an issue. It's a guy's sport, and [the men players] felt like Katie was forced on them. It was obvious Katie was not very good. She was awful."[128] The "Katie was forced on them" line was especially poetic given the circumstances. (Barnett told *SB Nation* in 2015, "No matter how good or bad Katie was, we wanted her to be a part of the program. Nobody even saw the compassion that was there."[129])

Hnida, who had since transferred to the University of New Mexico, said she came forward because of "the recent allegations into the football program" at CU. While she was talking about the other women who had reported players, she was also talking about a bevy of accusations that included a report by Keenan's office saying the athletic department specifically used sex and alcohol to recruit.[130] There were rumors of hired escorts and strippers being used during recruitment. Barnett was suspended for his comments about Hnida.

On the heels of Hnida's interview revealing her assault, police announced two more cases that were under investigation, one from September 2001 and another from August 2002.[131] In the former case, the woman said that Barnett had told her if she pressed charges, he would back his player.

Barnett's suspension ended in late May 2004. The athletic director resigned in November 2004. The president of the university resigned in March 2005. Barnett agreed to leave in December of that year.

In the middle of it all, the NCAA claimed it was finally going to do something about the problems with out-of-control recruitment.

IV.

The NCAA's master move: "The Shrug." The Gator Getters/ Guides were under scrutiny in 2004 in the wake of what happened at Colorado. Many schools were reconsidering using all-female or mostly female host groups. UF had its own particular case unfolding. The *Sun* reported that top recruit Willie Williams had a "turbulent visit to Gainesville" in late January 2004.[132] "During his two-night stay in Gainesville, Williams is alleged by police to have fondled a female student, punched a man in the face at a nightclub, and set off three fire extinguishers in his hotel—all within a five-hour period."

Williams, nicknamed "The Killer" and "Da Predator" in high school, visited three other schools that year: Florida State, Auburn, and Miami. The *Miami Herald* asked Williams to keep a recruitment diary during his visits. In a 2014 article at *Bleacher Report*, Jeff Pearlman reviewed these diary entries in an article titled, "The Tragic Story of Willie Williams, College Football's First Celebrity Recruit."[133] In the Auburn entry, Williams said the hostesses were "there to cheer you up" but he wasn't smitten with them. What Williams really enjoyed was the party on campus he went to at night with his host. "The girls at the party were much better than the farmer girls we'd see all day around campus. I was kind of worried all Auburn had to offer was those farmer girls that talked funny. But the girls at the party weren't farmer girls at all. I thought they must have bused them in from Miami." During his Miami trip, which took place in his hometown, the events were capped off on South Beach where "they took us to this place called 'The Bed.' Warren Sapp, Clinton Portis, Jevon Kearse, and a whole bunch of really hot girls were all there." Florida was his last stop. He casually mentioned, "They had girls come out, all dressed nice, but it took awhile."

Williams got probation and community service (he had been on probation for an earlier offense at the time of his UF visit). He went on to play ball at Miami but his career fizzled while there.

The overlap between recruitment and violence against women simply can't be ignored when teams are obviously using women-as-prizes-for-attending-a-university as part of their recruitment strategy. These cases of sexual assault and football recruitment illustrate how, all too often, the protective culture of men's college athletics in Division I can be harmful. Perhaps the best example is that of Nigel Clay, one of two Oklahoma football players found guilty of gang-raping a woman in a dormitory in 1989. In 1992, Clay told the *Los Angeles Times*, "I don't know how to say it, but, bottom line, I just felt that sometimes, walking around . . . Well, speaking for myself and a lot of other people, we felt like we were above the law, like OU would protect us from anything."[134]

Barry Switzer, Clay's coach at the time, when talking to the *New York Times* in 2002 about the kind of recruitment parties where the women in the December 2001 Colorado case say they were raped, explained, "There are groupies everywhere and sex is going to happen when kids are involved."[135] You can practically see Switzer shrugging as he said that.

When looking at how the NCAA handled the issue of recruitment following the news out of Colorado, one can easily imagine them shrugging too.

The national reaction to the events at Colorado led the NCAA to set up a Task Force on Recruiting that made recommendations to the organization's Division I Board of Directors. According to a July 20, 2004, NCAA press release, one of those recommendations was:

> *Member institutions must develop written policies for official recruiting visits to be approved by the president or chancellor. The policies would apply to prospective student-athletes, student hosts, coaches, and other athletics administrators. Among other things, the policies must prohibit the use of alcohol, drugs, sex, and gambling in recruiting. Colleges and*

universities must submit their official and unofficial visit policies to their conference offices by December 1, 2004. Institutions independent of conferences must submit their policies to the NCAA national office. The policies must be reviewed every four years by an outside entity. Under this measure, the NCAA reserves the right to investigate major violations of recruiting policy.

In August 2004, the NCAA press release was more vague: "Campuses must develop written policies that specifically prohibit inappropriate or illegal behavior in recruiting. Policies must be approved by campus presidents or chancellors by December 1, and be on file with conference offices."

What ended up in the Division I manual is:

An institution must have written departmental policies related to official visits that apply to prospective student-athletes, student hosts, coaches, and other athletics administrators that are approved by the institution's president or chancellor and kept on file at the institution and conference office. The institution is responsible for the development and enforcement of appropriate policies and penalties regarding specified areas, as identified by the NCAA Division I Board of Directors. The institution shall have an outside entity (e.g., conference office) evaluate its policies related to official visits once every four years. The institution may be held accountable through the NCAA infractions process for activities that clearly demonstrate a disregard for its stated policies.

You'll notice that the "prohibit the use of alcohol, drugs, sex, and gambling" wording is not there.

Then there is one other rule that matters here, the one about student hosts. The manual states, "The student host must be either a current student-athlete or a student designated in a manner consistent with the institution's policy for providing campus visits or tours to prospective students in general." In other words, whatever a school's overall policy is for showing any prospective student around campus must be mirrored in what the athletic department does. If your student hosts on campus aren't mainly women, then your students hosts for athletics cannot be either. It is this rule, combined with the written policies, that have seemingly ended student host programs for athletics that are mainly populated by women.

Not to put too fine a point on it, but nowhere explicitly in the Division I manual does it say that teams cannot use women and/or sex for recruitment. Perhaps people feel this would be unnecessary and redundant, but a lot has happened since 2004 to suggest otherwise.

V.

If schools were supposed to give up their all-female recruitment groups or to stop using women in a particular way in recruitment following the revelations at Colorado, some of them apparently did not get the NCAA's memo.

In 2009, Tennessee, then coached by Lane Kiffin, came under fire when it was revealed that female hostesses had driven to a high school football game in South Carolina and held up signs saying, *Come to Tennessee.* Three Tennessee recruits were playing that night. Recruiting players off campus is a violation.

In a *New York Times* piece about the recruiting scandal, Marcus Lattimore, a running back who went on to play at South Carolina, said, "You don't want to go to a college where they ain't pretty."[136] Christian Jones, a linebacker who attended Florida State, also talked about texting with hostesses from Tennessee: "That's real exciting, getting people like that wanting to support you."

Lacey Pearl Earps, a former hostess at Tennessee and one of the women at the center of that high school–visit scandal, told Jeff Benedict and Armen Keteyian, the authors the 2013 book, *The System: The Glory and Scandal of Big-Time College Football*, "The only inappropriate thing we did was lead on seventeen- and eighteen-year-old guys just to get them to come to the school." She went on: "We are not the only ones who do that. That goes on with hostesses at lots of schools. And no one tells us to do that. We just did it."[137]

Benedict and Keteyian argue that leading these young men on with "the promise of an intimate relationship is the sort of thing that can trump sold-out stadiums, state-of-the-art facilities, Nike deals, and schedules packed with nationally televised games." Even though Earps says that no one in college football programs tells hostesses to "lead on" recruits, programs are well aware of how instrumental these women are in helping them land top athletes. Benedict and Keteyian write, "Even the NCAA has very little in the way of regulations to keep hostesses in check . . . For the most part, hostesses are a part of the system that gets very little scrutiny."

The publication of Benedict and Keteyian's book on the seedy side of big-time college athletics coincided with a September 2013 five-part series at *Sports Illustrated* that focused primarily on the culture of the Oklahoma State University football program.[138] After covering money, academics, and drugs, reporters George Dohrmann and Thayer Evans (with help from Melissa Segura) turned their attention to sex and the Orange Pride, the OSU hostess group.

Yes, in 2013, OSU still had an all-female hostess group it used in football recruitment.

At that time, the website for the Orange Pride said that members are "required to attend and work each home football game for the 2013 football season, raise $300 in sponsorship money, attend weekly meetings, and work recruiting official visits, Junior Days, Coaches Clinic, etc." The *SI* piece said that between 2001 and 2011, a small number of women in Orange Pride slept with recruits while they were visiting campus. It also says that members of the OSU football staff "decided which hostess to pair with which recruits" and "were aware that certain Orange Pride members were having sex with visiting prospects." Also, "Oklahoma State football personnel played a central role in vetting Orange Pride candidates." In the feature, Artrell Woods, a former OSU player, told the magazine, "There's no other way a female can convince you to come play football at a school besides [sex]. The idea was to get [recruits] to think that if they came [to Oklahoma State], it was gonna be like that all the time, with . . . girls wanting to have sex with you."

The scandal appeared to be that the football program did not do enough to prohibit sex during recruiting and thus broke NCAA rules. Not quite.

In late April 2015, the NCAA, following up on *Sports Illustrated*'s series, announced that OSU had violated recruitment policies with their Orange Pride hostess program. Specifically, the infraction was that the football program controlled the hostess program, so it did not serve all students at the university. Hosts or hostesses of student-athletes either have to be "a current student-athlete," the infraction decision reads, "or a student who is designated in a manner consistent with the institution's policies for providing campus tours or visits to prospective students in general." The infraction decision specifically states that "gender-based student hosting groups was impermissible," but when I asked the NCAA's associate director of public and media relations, Emily James, if the fact that it was all-female broke the NCAA's rules specifically or just the university's rules, I did not get a response. She did tell me, though, "NCAA rules do not allow the use of student hosts in a way that is inconsistent with the university's policies on providing campus tours or visits to all prospective students."

The other curious part of the NCAA infraction decision is the part where it lists the "impermissible hosting activities" that the investigators discovered at OSU: "They accompanied prospects to on-campus and off-campus meals, participated in campus tour activities, and interacted with prospects in the team dining area." Since this investigation was to the NCAA's admission spurred on by the *SI* report, the lack of sex among the impermissible activities is strange. It's especially strange if the NCAA bans "the use of alcohol, drugs, sex, and gambling in recruiting." (Apparently it does not.) It's possible they found no evidence of sex in recruitment. When I asked the NCAA for clarification on this point, I got nearly the same verbatim response from James: OSU, for the NCAA, was about inconsistency in university versus athletic department policies.

This is important, whether the NCAA bans using women and sex in this particular way. For now, it looks like the problem for the NCAA is the boring and legalistic consistency issue. Not, as the assistant athletic director at Notre Dame described it in 2003, that athletic departments are selling sex to attract high school recruits to their campuses.

What does this mean then for a school like Vanderbilt?

In August 2013, four Vanderbilt football players were charged with sexually assaulting a fellow student.[139] The woman had met one of the defendants during recruitment. At the trial for two of the players, Cory Batey and Brandon Vandenburg, Vandenburg's lawyers asked multiple witnesses—friends of the woman and some former players—if they knew of a "hostess" program under James Franklin, the head coach at the time of the reported rape. While no witness admitted knowing of such a program, it was no surprise that Vandenburg's lawyers asked about it. According to the local Nashville paper the *Tennessean*, "The woman told police she was at a medical examination four days after the incident when [then–head coach Franklin] and [then–director of performance enhancement Dwight] Galt told her they 'cared about her because she assisted them with recruiting.'" According to a court filing, what she meant by "assisting them with recruiting" was that Franklin asked her "to get fifteen pretty girls together and form a team to assist with the recruiting even though he knew it was against the rules."

Vanderbilt's vice chancellor for public affairs, Beth Fortune, responded to this filing with the following statement: "Vanderbilt University's Athletics Department does not have a hostess program. The Athletics Department adheres to NCAA policies governing prospective student-athlete visits to campus and the Athletics Department's own Recruiting Policy for Official and Unofficial Visits." Tom Thurman, the deputy DA in the case, told the *Philadelphia Inquirer* that Franklin called the victim as a show of support, not "for any purpose of covering up or anything like that." He also said he believed Franklin knew her because she had an association with the athletic department.

According to people in the Nashville community, some of them former students, there are many rumors about Franklin asking members of Vanderbilt's dance and cheerleading teams to help with recruitment in ways that fall outside of school-sanctioned events—but no one would talk to me about them on the record. So-called hostess programs like the one rumored under Franklin are not uncommon at big-time sports programs, but since they are frowned upon, they are rarely discussed publicly. Ashlyn Alongi, who was involved in recruiting as a cheerleader, told me "there are so many rumors" about what recruitment was like under Franklin, but that none of them are true. If anything like what Vandenburg's lawyers have alleged did happen, she said, "it wouldn't have been through the athletic office."

Franklin has come under fire in the past for sexist comments he made in the spring of 2012 to a radio show host. When explaining one criteria for how he selects assistant coaches, Franklin commented, "I've been saying it for a long time, I will not hire an assistant until I see his wife. If she looks the part and she's a D1 recruit, then you got a chance to get hired. That's part of the deal."[140] Kaka Ray, a Nashville crisis management and prevention specialist who works with athletes, says that when she heard those remarks she felt like "this whole thing is going to implode, because if he is giving that to the press, what must have he been giving to his players?"

Thad McHaney, a defensive end and defensive tackle who played under Franklin and then was a student-coach alongside him, says that after he first heard about the incident and the charges against his fellow players, he was shocked and disappointed. But he cautions, "I never made the correlation that just because we are doing better in football we have people that are going to do that sort of thing." And he says that making the leap from football to sexual violence would be unjust to his former coach: "I think that's not fair to what [Franklin's] taught us as far as respecting women."

The trial in 2015 happened to coincide with that year's annual NCAA-sanctioned forty-eight-hour recruitment visit. Three of the players (including Batey) attended the same recruitment weekend in 2012 (all three were redshirted their freshmen year) and Vandenburg the one in 2013. The *Tennessean* reported that during 2014's recruitment visit, a seventeen-year-old recruit was accused of raping a Vanderbilt student.[141] The allegations were deemed "unfounded" after a police investigation, but "heavy underage drinking was documented by police and witnesses."

Franklin left Vanderbilt for Penn State in 2014. Asked for comments through the Penn State Athletic Communications Department, Franklin issued this statement: "The allegations that I did something wrong are simply not true. I have cooperated fully with the authorities in this matter but, out of respect for the legal process, I am not able to comment any further." Batey and Vandenburg were convicted but then the judge ruled there was a mistrial and threw out the convictions. Batey was retried in April 2016 and found guilty of aggravated rape, facilitation of aggravated rape, two counts of attempted aggravated rape, and three counts of aggravated sexual battery. Vandenburg is slated to go back to court in June 2016. No trial date has been set for the other two.

And no word on whether Vanderbilt or Franklin will face any finger-wagging from the NCAA.

Meanwhile, for Army, using women in recruitment as lures for potential players meant nothing to the NCAA in 2014. In October that year, the head coach there accepted responsibility for a recruiting trip that had happened earlier in the year.[142] An internal report found that "Army football recruiters use female cadets to help sell West Point." In fact, it was West Point's director of football operations who "recruited cheerleaders and members of the academy's women's basketball and volleyball teams to act as dinner dates for recruits." It was important, the director said to the women, that they participate because, "We want recruits to see that there are pretty girls that go here," and, "There are not just masculine women that attend West Point."

The NCAA, in typical fashion, slapped the Army's wrist.

West Point got a warning that they'd get in trouble the next time something like this happens.

As always, the NCAA shrugged.

VI.

Here's one last matter to question about the NCAA's role in all of this: shouldn't they at least care about other athletes?

Katie Hnida, the former Colorado kicker who came forward in 2004, is now a public figure who speaks often about her experiences as a sexual assault survivor, works with teams to bring further attention to this issue, and helps other survivors looking for comfort and assistance. She is one of the most well-known college football sexual assault survivors—and when she was assaulted, she was an NCAA player too.

Sasha Menu Courey, a swimmer at Missouri, was an athlete when she reported her assault. So was the woman who reported Travis Johnson at FSU; she was a shot-putter on the track team. So was a woman who accused a Baylor football player of rape in 2013; she was a soccer player. It's not uncommon for athletes to report other athletes for sexual assault: they share the same space repeatedly, come in contact often.

The NCAA never sanctioned Colorado for what happened under Barnett.

In 2007, the university settled a Title IX lawsuit and paid $2.8 million total to Lisa Simpson and another woman who said that they were raped at a party attended by CU football players.[143]

It was announced in July 2013 that the University of Colorado was facing a Title IX lawsuit. In May 2014, the school settled the lawsuit for $32,500 and did not admit liability or fault. The federal Title IX investigation is ongoing.

In December 2014, Gary Barnett told the *Denver Post*, "By

the end of my tenure, we had gone through allegations that were unfounded and recruiting issues that were never substantiated. Nevertheless, it created unrest around our program that made it very difficult to recruit and compete with the likes of Oklahoma and Texas in the Big 12."[144]

In January 2015, the University of Colorado suspended a player after a woman reported that he cornered her in a dorm room and sexually assaulted her, touching her without her consent.[145] According to the *Daily Camera*, the student-run paper for CU, the police report said that she "woke up . . . to the feeling of breath on her face and neck, and she could feel the sensation of someone next to her." She says he then groped her while she acted like she was asleep, "hoping that the touching would stop and that he would go away."

And then in August 2015, Barnett returned to Colorado.[146] He is their new color commentator for the radio broadcast of their games. Upon hiring Barnett, the athletic director told the local news, "Certainly, we know what's happened in the past. Our focus is on the future and what's best for CU now and in the future. We looked around and we all came to the same conclusion—that Gary Barnett was the best hire." The question isn't whether Colorado knows what happened, it's whether they care.

It looks like nothing's changed.

To be fair, the NCAA did publish a new handbook in September 2014 titled "Addressing Sexual Assault and Interpersonal Violence: Athletics' Role in Support of Healthy and Safe Campuses."[147] While the title is dry, the content is actually very strong. It should be required reading for all student-athletes, but also everyone who works in athletics. Yet, there's a significant problem with this handbook: it's not enforceable. It's a great resource of information and an impressive set of preventive measures that athletic departments can implement if they want to.

If the NCAA is going to continue to allow athletic departments to use women to recruit while simultaneously shrugging at the problem of sexual assault, we have to think about what that means for other athletes, especially female ones. Who, really, does the NCAA exist to protect and which players do they actually care about?

Moving On

I.

Sports media are old hats at adopting familiar narratives to discuss yet another athlete being accused of sexual violence. There are two go-to plays in the media's section of the college football sexual violence playbook: 1) advocate for moving on from the case as soon as possible; and 2) minimize the violence, often effectively erasing it from the story altogether. There are plenty of moments where variations on those plays end up combining the two. There are times, even, where reporting ventures into dangerous territory, where ethical lines are skirted in order to get a story.

Any member of the media will explain to you how important media is in shaping cultural narratives. If the sports media truly believe that, then it's time to alter the old playbook. Your plays, my fellow colleagues, are bad.

II.

The most overused play in the media's playbook: "Moving On." There is nothing sports media love more than when a high-profile case about off-field violence seemingly comes to end and we can all just move on. They practically beg us all to get back to the truly important stuff: talking about the minutiae of the sport that happens on the field.

Take, for example, this abbreviated news cycle in October 2014.[148] The University of Florida announced on a Monday that freshman quarterback Treon Harris was under investigation by the UFPD for sexual battery because a female student had reported that he sexually assaulted her.[149] Harris was immediately placed on an indefinite suspension from the team and barred from the school's campus.

But within hours of the suspension, a local college reporter was tweeting damning rumors about the woman using an anonymous source.[150] Three days later, Harris's lawyer, Huntley Johnson, released a letter detailing Harris's side of the story, in which Johnson called the woman a "sexual aggressor" and chronicled her supposed interaction with Harris leading up to the incident in question. The next day, the woman dropped her complaint (which tells us nothing about Harris's innocence or guilt or what the truth is in this particular case). Harris was reinstated on Friday. And by Sunday, *Bleacher Report* was asking, "Can Treon Harris Save Will Muschamp's Job?"[151] while Gatorsports.com wrote that Harris is "looking forward to moving on."

And Harris moved on. In 2015, after the starting QB for UF got a one-year suspension for using performance-enhancing drugs, Harris took over that top spot.

But these cases are so rarely about the individual people involved. Instead, they tell larger stories about power on campuses and in communities. Because Harris and UF football were ready to move on, that doesn't mean the questions are all answered. If Harris is no longer the center of this story, we might instead ask: What do we know about how the University of Florida treats sexual assault victims? How does racism function in Gainesville? What relationship does the UF athletic department have with the UFPD, if any? (Especially considering the way things have gone at rival FSU; see Chapter 3.) Who is Huntley Johnson and why has Mike Bianchi called him "the 1972 Dolphins of criminal defense attorneys when it comes to erasing potential legal problems for University of Florida athletes"?[152]

So the sport media go, though. When cases like this—athletes accused of committing violent crimes against women—come to their legal end, we hear a lot of speculation about what the case will mean for the player, his team, his school, his league. On December 5, 2013, within hours of Florida state attorney Willie Meggs announcing that he would not be pressing charges against Florida State's star quarterback, Jameis Winston, Gregg Doyel, a national columnist with CBS Sports, posted a piece titled "After State Declined Chance to Judge Winston, Time for Us to Follow Suit."[153] Doyle opened the piece with these bold, unequivocal statements: "The state of Florida did its job in the Jameis Winston case. Interviewed the victim, tested DNA, talked to witnesses. The state of Florida did its job and concluded that it doesn't have enough to charge the Florida State quarterback with rape. Now it's our turn to do our job—and respect that decision." It's a good guess that when Doyel wrote that "our job" was now to move on and "respect that decision," he was probably directing his remarks to journalists and media pundits, though possibly the public at large.

Moving on, though, is not necessarily what the media should be doing. Walt Bogdanich of the *New York Times* didn't heed Doyel's request. On April 16, 2014, Bogdanich penned a long, damning piece about the poor job the state of Florida did when it came to interviewing the victim and talking to witnesses.[154] "Officer Angulo's investigation was halting at best," Bogdanich writes of the main Tallahassee Police Department investigator on the case. He describes the weaknesses in Angulo's work as "confound[ing] prosecutors" and "mudd[ying] the outcome of the case." And that work was signed off by Angulo's superiors in the department. FSU faired as poorly in the piece: "The *Times*' examination—based on police and university records, as well as interviews with people close to the case, including lawyers and sexual assault experts—found that, in the Winston case, Florida State did little to determine what had happened." In fact, Bogdanich argues, "University administrators, in apparent violation of federal law, did not promptly investigate either the rape accusation or the witness's admission that he had videotaped part of the encounter."

Doyel wrote that those who continue to care about the Winston case are being unfair "to Jameis Winston, to the system we have, to the state of Florida for spending time and money to pursue the accuser's story before deciding, no, there just isn't a case there." I understand the impulse to move the spotlight off the players when they legal system moves on. That notion is quite possibly grounded in a desire to protect a legally innocent person from a narrative that questions their character. But this brings up two points. First, this is yet another example of the limits of basing how we talk about violence almost exclusively on how the law and courts handle it. Very few cases are as simple as what the law demands of them, and no matter the legal outcome, communities will have to find some way to manage with a potentially dangerous person and a potentially victimized one in them. Second, that impulse by writers, journalists, and editors to be fair to the player is why the entire discussion around this issue has to de-center the athlete. When the story we tell about a systemic violence is about an individual, it makes it too easy to gloss over the larger context and to ignore the reality that it will not be long before we are talking once more about another individual and the perpetuation of this violence.

There is a fundamental difference in the way that Doyel and Bogdanich approached the case, one that allowed Doyel to immediately—within hours of the announcement of no charges being pressed—decide to move on, and one that led Bogdanich to spend the next five months working on understanding the failures that played a role in the absence of charges. Bogdanich de-centered the athlete and centered the woman in his piece, while Doyel never mentions her, except in those first sentences when he notes that she was interviewed. You'll note that Doyel, when he listed to whom we were being unfair by continuing to discuss the case, did not address the question of fairness with regard to the woman. In the Winston case, the woman had to leave campus and finish her courses remotely. At a press conference in December 2013, her attorney said, "Her life's been turned upside down."

You often hear an exhaustion in the words and voices of people who want others to just stop talking about cases they see as closed. But to have decided that the Winston case was closed on December 5, 2013, was to view it only from the perspective of the accused athlete.

This, in a nutshell, is one of the biggest issues with sports being the arena in which we, as a society, so often talk through our ideas about sexual assault: in sports, athletes are centered, even in stories where they are the alleged perpetrators of crimes. Those hired to talk about sports are paid to analyze plays and players' abilities, to make predictions about the outcome of upcoming games, and to explain the sport to a lay audience. That those same people are tasked with discussing the realities of violence in our everyday lives with any kind of nuance or attention to the victim is a problem that only serves to further marginalize victims. Part of the issue is that the sports media is overwhelmingly male and, as a December 2015 report by the Women's Media Center found, they mainly speak to men ("75 percent of quotes in sports content were from male sources.").

Only 7 percent of sports stories about campus sexual assault were written by women but overall, WMC found, women reporters use female sources more. And female sources tend "to speak about the impact of sexual assault on the alleged victim at a much higher rate than male sources."

It is hard to imagine a sports media that do not always focus on the athlete. But it is an intriguing idea, a goal to work toward perhaps. Because, in the end, de-centering the athlete is not only more fair to women who report, it is more fair to the players, as it draws attention away from the individual and instead forces us to interrogate the system itself.

III.

A go-to play for many sports writers: "The Easy Road." In August 2013, the sports media were inundated with stories that had titles like, "Source: Manziel Questioned by NCAA."[155] The Heisman-winning sophomore quarterback for Texas A&M, Johnny Manziel, was under investigation by the NCAA for possibly selling his autograph:

> *The real issue, though, is . . . whether Manziel or any other college athlete has the right to have any control over the value of his name. The NCAA investigation, which is far from a certain success, stems from Manziel's alleged violation of Bylaw 12.5.2.1, which prohibits athletes from making money for promoting or endorsing commercial products or services. In effect, it keeps them from monetizing their name or their status as a college athlete, whether through signing autographs or starting their own businesses or in any other way.*[156]

It's no exaggeration to say this was the biggest college football story going into that season. CBS got themselves a "Johnny Cam" to follow his every moment on the field to broadcast to fans and haters far and wide. Sports media latched onto this story, sank their claws deep, and tried to hold on until they had extracted every last drop of blood from it.

Fair enough. Manziel's play on the field and attitude off the field made him the most high-profile player during the 2012 season. He was the first freshman to ever win the Heisman. He led a team that has traditionally been middling into the toughest college football conference—the SEC—and shocked everybody by beating the number one team in all the land. Manziel was featured in the Heisman trophy pose on the cover of *Time* with the words, "It's Time to Pay College Athletes."

In the end, though, nothing ever came of it beyond simply being a media story.

Happening concurrently with the Manziel news was the unfolding of the Vanderbilt gang rape case involving four players (discussed in Chapter 4). The Vanderbilt story broke just before the Manziel one did, and while everyone was talking about Manziel, there was almost total silence about Vanderbilt in the national media beyond a short Associated Press article. Local Nashville media carried the water for the national media on that story for a very long time and continues to do so as the case stretches into 2016. There was also a trial happening involving multiple Navy football players charged with sexual assault of a midshipwoman.

It's not that sports media don't like controversy, it's that they like it packaged in ways so that if you removed the story from the world of sports, the story wouldn't matter. Manziel discussions were mainly about if he'd get in trouble with the NCAA and if we were at a turning point with paying college athletes, both interesting to sports media because they could be related directly to what would happen to play on the field. Maybe Manziel wouldn't be allowed to play or A&M, a team on the rise, would get punished. Or if Manziel did have an effect on paying college players, what would the impact of that be on athletic departments and on the game itself? Those stories are the easy road. Less often do stories about paying college football players venture into the weeds to highlight our cultural ideas about labor, whose labor we feel comfortable exploiting, or the long history of the NCAA's maneuvers to keep pay out of players' hands. Just like with sexual assault, the discussions about labor in college football are getting more robust, but it's no secret that sports media are much more comfortable whenever their sports stories stay primarily within the confines of the field.

On some level, the "media don't care about it" criticism is old and boring. So let me be clear: it's not that sexual assault cases are not covered by the media (though, sometimes that is true), it's that they are flash-in-the-pan takes (everyone is, after all, in a hurry to move on) compared to other stories that are less complicated, where the moral positioning is less stressful or controversial. By merely choosing to cover a story about an athlete accused of a crime, writers and journalists are often described as having agendas, the connotation being that the motivations must be sinister or malicious.

We should be having a conversation about paying collegiate athletes. But we also really need to be having a conversation about the intersection of sports and sexual violence. We have to figure out a way for both to take place at the same time. The easy road just isn't good enough.

IV.

One of the more hurtful plays the media run is "The Minimizer." Often when reading about these cases, you wouldn't know that any violence has been reported, the extent of it, the utter seriousness of the issue at hand.

Often this is a rhetorical exercise. In February 2015, Kavitha A. Davidson critiqued how the media covered Jameis Winston at the NFL Combine.[157] The piece begins: "Scouts and commentators are falling over themselves to laud Jameis Winston's performance at the NFL Combine. They're talking arm strength, 40 times, football IQ, interception rate, what have you. The only thing they're not talking about? Sexual assault." Davidson catalogs the many euphemisms that stand in for actually addressing the allegations of violence ("off-the-field issues," "behavioral problems," "character flaws," "immaturity," "bad decisions," "mistakes," "baggage"), but then shrewdly argues, "As many studies have noted, using euphemistic language to describe rape effectively downplays the seriousness of the issue. Victims have a hard enough time being taken seriously by the justice system. But the flippancy with which rape can be dismissed as a 'bad decision' has tangible consequences, allowing us to to keep things as they are without striving for meaningful reform." To drive the point home, Davidson ends all nine paragraphs in her piece with the phrase "sexual assault." She literally writes the violence back in. She was also very pointed about why sports reporters write like this: "These men really, really don't want to think of sexual violence when they think of Jameis Winston. They'd like to forget the accusations—for fans to forget too—and concentrate on important things like third-down conversions. It's far easier to envision your team drafting an immense talent when you don't associate him with sexual assault."

This shouldn't be a surprise, especially not with what we already knew about the media and the Winston case. Tomas Rios, writing at *Sports on Earth* in December 2013, just days after Florida state attorney Willie Meggs announced that there would be no charges filed against Jameis Winston, drew attention to the media's complicity in Florida State's desire to just avoid the topic altogether.[158] "In the twenty-two days between *TMZ* first reporting Winston as the suspect and the morbidly vaudevillian press conference which effectively closed the case," Rios writes, "FSU imposed a 'football questions only' decree on the media that was met with no resistance because countering PR machinations is no longer an important part of the media's job—assuming that it ever was." As Rios goes on to point out, media make these choices because of the fear of losing access to teams and players that are vital to their jobs. But, Rios says, "Here's the thing: access is a useless status symbol when its price is not asking the questions one should ask." He's right.

Sometimes, the minimizing comes in shocking forms. In September 2015, Jesse Leroy Matthew Jr. was indicted for murdering a Virginia Tech student, Morgan Harrington, in 2009. He was already accused of killing a University of Virginia student, Hannah Graham, in 2014. Part of Matthew's story was that he played football at Liberty University until 2002, his junior year, when he withdrew from the school after a fellow student reported that he had raped her. He then enrolled at Christopher Newport University and within a few weeks a student there said that he had raped her. He left that university soon after that. Forensic evidence now links him to the murders of Graham and Harrington, as well as a 2005 sexual assault in northern Virginia. In October 2014, the Associated Press ran an article about Matthew that started thusly: "Jesse Leroy Matthew Jr. was the kind of guy who would bust your lip, then regretfully drive you to the hospital. A 'cool individual' around other guys, but a bit too 'touchy-feely' with the ladies, family friend Rod Brown says. 'He doesn't mean to be creepy; he's just a little off, just a little awkward,' says Brown, who's known 'LJ' for about fifteen years. 'If he gets around women, I've never seen it NOT be awkward.'"[159] The AP chose to start the story of this man accused of two murders and three rapes with the euphemism "a bit too 'touchy-feely.'"

Then there is the "but he seems nice to me" minimizing tactic that no one should ever use. When James Franklin was hired away from Vanderbilt to Penn State in early 2014, some people were confused by this choice. It had only been six months since four of his players were arrested on charges of gang-raping a fellow student, and Penn State is now best known for their institutional cover-up of a former coach's rape of children. Dan Wolken, USA Today's national college football reporter, stated on a radio show in early January that Franklin was never discussed as a possible coach for the vacancy at USC because of the ongoing case against his former players.[160] Talking about Franklin's hire, Wolken said, "It [the case] is one reason why, frankly, I was surprised this [Franklin's hire] went down."

Gregg Doyel, in his CBS Sports column, said that Franklin was "perfect" for the Penn State job.[161] About the pending sexual assault case, Doyel wrote, "Look, I'm not going to dismiss or gloss over what happened there. That was a tragedy, what happened at Vanderbilt, and because it involved James Franklin's football program, it involved James Franklin." But, Doyel goes on, "Nothing about the way James Franklin has presented himself makes me think he did anything wrong at Vanderbilt." Well then. The reason Doyel prefaces the his statement about Franklin with "I'm not going to dismiss or gloss over what happened there" is because he knows what he is about to write probably does just that. The thing about these cases for those of us on the outside looking in: we don't know the people and we don't know what they did. But it's important to know that often, in order to justify not believing survivors, people say, "Well, he doesn't look like he did anything," or, "He's not acting like he did anything wrong." Those are loaded words that drain the seriousness out of the case and replace it with a gut feeling about a virtual stranger.

Another time "The Minimizer" pops up is when reporters are waxing nostalgic about a player or coach. In May 2015, Jeff Hauser at *SB Nation* wrote a piece about a former Colorado player, Brendan Schaub.[162] Schaub played at Colorado under head coach Gary Barnett (see Chapter 4). The very Barnett who, when he heard that a former athlete of his, Katie Hnida, had said a teammate of hers raped her while they both were playing for Barnett, told reporters, "It's a guy's sport, and [the men players] felt like Katie was forced on them. It was obvious Katie was not very good. She was awful." The same Barnett under whom multiple women came forward to report having been raped by football players. Hauser described it in his piece this way: "Like most of the players who come in contact with Barnett, they share the same opinion. Sadly, the reputation of the longtime coach became tarnished by the controversy during his time at CU. Several players on the football team were entangled in rape allegations, ultimately forcing Barnett to resign from the program in 2005." Hauser couldn't have said less, couldn't have sanitized or flattened the reality of what happened under Barnett any more than shoving it all into the phrase "rape allegations." "Rape allegations" that "sadly" "tarnished" Barnett's reputation. One wonders for whom it was sad.

Perhaps a more troubling version of this kind of writing came from Hauser later that year, in September 2015, after CU announced that Barnett would return to be the color commentator on the radio. In a piece titled "Gary Barnett Enthusiastic to Put the Past Behind Him at Colorado," Hauser writes that

Barnett was fired "following the controversy of sex abuse and recruiting scandals," but a few sentences later says that the firing led to "the start of the football program hitting rock bottom without any justification of wrongdoing," immediately launching into why that unexplained "controversy" really wasn't anything at all.[163] In the rest of the piece, Barnett gets space to explain how his comments about Hnida were taken out of context and "as it was played out, it was an attack on me and thinking I was attacking a female athlete. Which had nothing to do with the situation at all." No matter. "Barnett," Hauser assures us, "isn't dwelling on the past errors" (because why would he?). This is a prime example of an overlap of the "Moving On" play and "The Minimizer" at work in tandem.

The avoidance of even a discussion of violence does the same work as Doyel's "nothing to see here anymore, let's move on" piece: we don't have to talk about the impact of that violence. As Rios put it in December 2013, "The common framing of the victim was as an abstract distraction—ESPN on-air talent in particular is guilty of this tactic—and, in doing so, the victim was denied any measure of humanity or, perish the thought, empathy."

There will always be reporters who only focus on football and who steadfastly refuse to jeopardize their credentials and access for the chance to ask the questions that someone should be asking if they care at all about the morality of the sport they write about. These are choices, though. And these choices have consequences in a real world where victims of sexual violence read the very things you are writing.

V.

"What Ethics?" One of the biggest college football sexual assault cases over the last few years happened at Vanderbilt in the summer of 2013[164] (see Chapter 4). ABC's *20/20*, following the conclusion of the first trial in early 2015 of two of the men involved, made terrible ethical decisions that not only could jeopardize the well being of the woman who reported the assault but the case itself. This is the absolute worse thing journalism can do and it is the play that must never be run, that should be ripped out of all the playbooks, lit on fire, and burned away.

In the early morning of June 23, 2013, the Nashville deputy district attorney says then–Vanderbilt wide receiver Chris Boyd received a text message with a photo attached. It showed an unconscious twenty-one-year-old woman being sodomized. The sender of the text was Brandon Vandenburg, a tight end who had recently transferred from the College of the Desert in California. He was, according to ESPN, "the nation's No. 1 junior college tight end" at the time he committed to Vanderbilt, but like the other defendants, he had yet to play a down for the program. According to a statement by the deputy district attorney during a plea hearing for Boyd on September 13, 2013, Boyd "promptly deleted [Vandenburg's text] because he didn't want his girlfriend to see it."

The deputy DA said that Boyd texted back: *Tell ur boys to delete that [expletive]. I'm looking out for your ass.* He followed up with, *And tell your roommate he didn't see [expletive].* (The expletives were edited out of the DA's transcript of the text messages.)

Vandenburg then called Boyd and asked him to come to his dorm in Gillette Hall. According to the DA's statement, Vandenburg told Boyd "that the victim had been 'messed with in the hall' and sexually assaulted in the room, and he needed Mr. Boyd to come over." Vandenburg was there with three other football players: Cory Batey, Brandon Banks, and Jaborian McKenzie. During the trial, McKenzie testified that the three of them were "like brothers . . . We were best friends."

Vandenburg had only arrived in Nashville a few weeks earlier and barely knew Batey, Banks, and McKenzie. He had spotted Banks and McKenzie walking back from a middle-of-the-night food run; Batey met them just outside the dorm, and Vandenburg asked them to help him move the body of the unconscious woman to his room.

Vandenburg had met up with the woman at a local bar, the Tin Roof, earlier that night. She was about to enter her senior year. She testified that the two had seen each other several times in the two weeks prior to the assault. At the bar Vandenburg gave her multiple drinks, and after the fourth one, a blue drink she said he called a "California Long Island Iced Tea," she remembers almost nothing until she woke up the next morning around eight a.m. According to the DA's opening statement at trial, Vandenburg drove them in her car to his dorm. With Banks's help, he got her body into the elevator and onto the second floor. Batey and McKenzie joined them there.

In Vandenburg's dorm room, according to the testimony of multiple witnesses and video and photographic evidence uncovered by police from the players' cell phones and surveillance footage in the dorm, Batey raped the woman and Vandenburg, Banks, and McKenzie took pictures and videos of the incident. Vandenburg tried to join in but was unable to achieve an erection, which witnesses say he blamed on being high on cocaine. Prosecutors argued that Vandenburg facilitated the assault, passing out condoms, encouraging Banks to penetrate her with a water bottle, and flushing the condoms down the toilet later. Because aggravated rape is a "general intent crime," prosecutors needed to prove that Vandenburg intended to commit sexual assault and that the sexual assault occurred, but they did not need to prove that Vandenburg himself committed the act.

According to McKenzie's testimony during the trial, Batey

undressed the woman and then penetrated her with his fingers. Banks touched her and took photos of her. Vandenburg and Batey both slapped her buttocks a few times to see if she was going to wake up. Batey also urinated on her.

Vandenburg sent photos and videos of the assault to two friends in California. Later, prosecutors say, Vandenburg flew to California and destroyed both phones. But one of the men had already downloaded the files to his computer, and Nashville police recovered them. In exchange for their testimony in court, the friends were offered a lesser charge of attempted accessory after the fact, down from a felony count of tampering with evidence. One of the men took it immediately after testifying and will be on unsupervised probation for the next year.

According to a text Chris Boyd sent to Batey on June 24, after Boyd arrived on the scene, *Me Carta and Vanderwall [sic] and Vandenburg helped us move her out of the hallway.* While speculation arose that Boyd was referencing Austyn Carta-Samuels in that text, the deputy district attorney said Boyd was wrong and Carta-Samuels, then the starting quarterback, was not there that night, and his name did not come up at trial. "Vanderwall" referred to tight end Dillon van der Wal, who was present in the dorm, but against whom the DA chose not to press charges. Boyd was not called to testify, though he had agreed to if he was. Van der Wal did testify. He, along with Michael Retta, a Vanderbilt tennis player, said they saw the woman lying unconscious in the hallway. DeAndre Woods, a football player who had just arrived on campus, helped Boyd move the woman's body from the hallway into the bed. Mack Prioleau, Vandenburg's roommate, was also there that night, asleep in his bed when the players arrived. He saw the woman on the floor, facedown, and he heard the other men talking about sex and what he said sounded like porn. Prioleau later slipped out of the room and went to sleep in a friend's room. None of these men called the police or reported what they saw to any official.

Boyd also texted his girlfriend that night to give her an update: *I got everything cleared up and I talked to both Tip [McKenzie] and Corey already. Deleted everything. She didn't remember [expletive] and feels bad.* In the days following the assault, according to the DA, Boyd "participated in a meeting with the four defendants involved in the case at a Popeyes chicken restaurant, where the case was discussed."

The woman woke up in a strange bed and didn't realize where she was until she wandered into the hall. She felt "out of it, I didn't feel like myself," she testified. She was "confused," "sick," "nauseous," had pain in her left shoulder and wrist, and her right knee was bleeding. She found vomit in her hair. There were bruises on her legs and her buttocks. She eventually went back to her apartment, never realizing what had happened to her.

It took two days before word of the incident made it to the Vanderbilt police department, after Vanderbilt housing staffers viewed surveillance footage from that night while investigating vandalism of the dorm. What they found—including video of the unconscious woman being dragged around, men entering and leaving the dorm room, and, at one point, Vandenburg covering the surveillance camera with a towel—prompted them to turn the tape over to police.

James Franklin, then Vanderbilt's head football coach, testified in October at a pretrial hearing that he was vacationing in Florida when he was told about the incident. He quickly flew back, but upon arriving in Nashville was instructed by the school's legal staff to "stay out of it." He held a team meeting, though, where he told the players he had seen video of the incident; he said at that same pretrial hearing that he had lied to his players and had "spoke as if I had seen the video because I was angry and upset and didn't want to water down the message to them."

When the police contacted the woman on June 26, three days after the assault, she says that she at first told them what Vandenburg had told her had happened: In the afternoon on the day of the assault, "he told me that I had gotten sick in his room and he had to clean it up and that it was horrible and that he had to spend the night taking care of me and it was horrible." In response to hearing this, she said, "I apologized. I was embarrassed." Later, when Vandenburg told her he feared that he and his teammates "might get kicked off the football team" because he was "getting blamed for stuff that didn't happen," she vowed to help him clear his name. The following day, though, she went for a medical exam.

By June 29 the four players had been dismissed from the team. On July 17 the athletic department barred Vanderbilt student-athletes from patronizing the Tin Roof. (David Williams, the vice chancellor for Athletics and University Affairs, later told the local media that it was not related to the June 23 incident, but rather that "he worried that student-athletes were being given free drinks—a possible violation of NCAA rules.")

On August 9, Vandenburg, Batey, McKenzie, and Banks were all indicted on charges of aggravated rape and sexual battery. Vandenburg was charged additionally with a count of unlawful photography and tampering with evidence. All of the players pleaded not guilty to all charges. Boyd was suspended from the team when he was indicted as an accessory after the fact. He pleaded guilty to the charge in mid-September 2013.

In October 2013, the district attorney announced that the cases of McKenzie and Banks would be separated from Vandenburg and Batey, meaning that two joint trials would take place.

While both Banks and McKenzie were expected to testify at trial, only McKenzie did. He hopes to get a plea deal.

The trial was finally held in January 2014 after a series of delays. It lasted twelve days. On January 27, the Nashville jury convicted Batey and Vandenburg on multiple counts of sexual battery and aggravated rape. It only took them three hours to come to that conclusion.

Then, on January 30, 2015, *20/20* dedicated an hour to detailing the police investigation and the trial. The program aired the surveillance footage from Gillette Hall on the night of the rape, marking the first time the public had seen it. During the trial, all videos and photographs were displayed so that only the jury, witnesses, lawyers, and judge could see them, because of the court's protective order on the material and considering that there were more defendants to try.

20/20 also aired an image during the East Coast broadcast of one of the indictments from the case file; in doing so, the news program briefly displayed the name of the victim on screen.

Julie Townsend, the senior vice president of communication for ABC News, says that the airing of the woman's name was a "terrible mistake" that "should never have happened." The program altered the West Coast broadcast to remove her name, had it removed from all online versions of the program, and apologized immediately to the woman through her attorney. They also launched an investigation to find out how the name made it on screen and "to make sure that never happens again."

As for airing a video that is still under the court's protective order, Townsend says that there were "extensive, serious conversations" about it before they showed it and that they feel they used it "extremely judiciously." It is not clear where ABC News obtained the video, and most parties involved in the case have denied culpability. Nashville District Attorney Glenn Funk issued the following statement to SI.com:

> *The District Attorney's Office is outraged that this video has been leaked. It is a violation of the court's protective order, another attack on the victim, and it could impact the co-defendants' right to a fair trial. Every member of the prosecution team is willing to testify, under oath, that the leak did not come from this office. We challenge the defense counsel to do the same. Further, the District Attorney's Office will cooperate and assist with any investigation by the court into this serious breach.*

Worrick Robinson, Batey's attorney, said that he and his colleague Liz Powers "are 100 percent confident that no case material from our office was given to ABC News or *20/20*... We are happy to accept the challenge by District Attorney Glenn Funk to testify under oath regarding any question the court may have about the video footage. I was just as surprised as others to see the surveillance and interrogation tapes" involved in the trial that aired on national TV.

Fletcher Long, Vandenburg's attorney at the time, told local Nashville news that he didn't "know how *20/20* got it" but that he "won't bite on the DA's offer to take oath."

There was no benefit to the public that justifies *20/20*'s decision to air that video. The ethics behind *20/20*'s editorial decisions were hard enough to understand when the trial was over. But, it turns out, the trial is not actually over. In June 2015, Vandenburg and Batey's convictions were overturned after the judge declared a mistrial due to an issue with the jury.[165]

Both were released from jail. Batey was retried in April 2016 and found guilty again. Vandenburg will go to trial in

June 2016. For Vandenburg's retrial, the judge decided to pull the jury from Memphis because of the high-profile nature of the case.

Hopefully none of them watched *20/20*.

VI.

In September 2013, during ESPN's *College Game Day*, a Michigan fan held up a sign that read, *Hi Lizzy Seeberg*. Seeberg had committed suicide in 2010 after she reported that a Notre Dame football player had sexually assaulted her and then, she said, his teammates threatened her.

People were angry about the sign. And *Deadspin* published a letter sent by the man who supposedly held the sign, in which he explained his reason for doing it: "We're here, Notre Dame. The story is out, and there's plenty of people who know about it and want change. You can't run forever."[166] We can argue over the semantics of the sign (like, for instance, that he should have chosen *RIP* instead of the much more creepy *Hi*), but there's a larger point here. Someone told me that day on Twitter, "Sadly that is the most coverage that story has gotten on ESPN." And that's probably true, except for maybe *Outside the Lines*. The sign might have been a poor choice but the problem its holder was trying to highlight is very real.

The media are as much a product of the sentiment around these cases as a force in shaping them. And it's that latter part— the ability to shape narratives and to give cultural conversations direction—that can't be ignored any longer by sports reporters who are going to write on topics like interpersonal violence, rape, or sexual violence. To continue to ignore this is to continue to perpetuate a harmful environment that props up questionable and even dangerous behavior and sidelines victims— sometimes, as *20/20* did in Nashville, literally jeopardizing the case. Because while players, teams, schools, and fans want to move forward, that can be much harder to do for the people reporting the violence.

Time to get some new, better plays for this old, damaging playbook.

PART II

How It Could Be

We know now what the old playbook looks like. We need a new one. I need a new one. What follows is not an exhaustive list of new plays we could or should adopt moving forward, but they are a start. And we have to start somewhere.

PLAY #1

Consent Is Cool; Get Some

The first play in this new playbook has to be about consent because we just don't talk about it enough. Honestly, it's hard to imagine that we could talk about it too much. So, let's get started.

After Oregon destroyed Florida State 59–20 in the semifinal of the college football playoffs in January 2015, some Oregon players mockingly threw the FSU tomahawk hand gesture and gleefully chanted, "No means no!" to the tune of FSU's fight song.[167] A reporter for FOX Sports captured a vine of it, and it traveled like wildfire through the Internet.

Everyone assumes they were referring to Jameis Winston (how could they have been referring to anything else?). This was FSU's first loss under Winston since he became starting quarterback at the beginning of the 2013 season. The response to the taunt ranged widely from criticism over Oregon making light of sexual violence to praise for the Duck players bringing attention to this particular issue when most of sports media barely even mentioned it.

At ESPN, Kate Fagan wrote:

In that context, the Oregon players seem to be using rape, and consent, as the fuel for some trash talking against a beaten opponent. In that context, the moment no longer

seems like a strong stand by a few socially conscious ath-
letes. In that context, the chant seems tasteless, further
trivializing sexual assault, which is actually a very serious
problem on college campuses, including at Oregon. In that
context, "No means no" is being wielded as a joke, a way
to gloat.[168]

I agree with her. I said so publicly on Twitter that night.
(Fagan included one of my tweets in the post, where I had
typed, "Important moment to remind everyone that rape isn't
a joke so don't make rape jokes, not about Winston or anyone
ever. KTHNXBAI.")

In response to the video going viral, Oregon head coach
Mark Helfrich wrote in a statement, "We are aware of the inappropriate behavior in the postgame. This is not what our
programs stand for, and the student-athletes will be disciplined
internally." There were people who were angry at Oregon for
this decision, noting the irony that Winston had never been
punished but the Oregon team that mocked him would be. At
Jezebel, Anna Merlan agreed with UO's decision. "These dudes,"
Merlan wrote, "were gloating, and they used an anti-rape chant
to do it. This is what trivializing sexual assault looks like, just in
case we needed yet another reminder."

There was a particular strain of criticism to this punishment,
especially from Oregon Duck fans (though not exclusively, of
course), that asked why it was wrong for the Oregon players
to support the woman in the Winston case, especially as they
were reinforcing the idea that consent is important. There were
plenty of people who did not care about either team who saw it
as an overall good—that on one of the biggest sports stages, in
the glow of a major victory, football players were speaking out
against sexual assault.

This issue of consent in the Winston case was front and center. Only days before, the transcript from Winston's disciplinary hearing had been released by the media. (I was one of them, having written a post about it at *Vice Sports* to which we attached the entire 214-page document.[169]) One of the things that was revealed for the first time was what Winston remembers about Kinsman giving consent that night. He read from a statement in which he said, "[Kinsman] had the capacity to consent to having sex with me, and she repeatedly did so by her conduct and verbal expressions." The judge overseeing the hearing pushed him on this point, asking Winston how he knew that Kinsman was consenting. Winston responded, "Verbally and physically." When pressed to explain what that consent looked and sounded like, Winston replied, "Moaning is mostly physically. Well, moaning is physically. And verbally at that time, Your Honor." Moaning. It is about the most vague answer that Winston could have given to that question. Kinsman, for her part, told the judge, "I remember pleading with him to stop clearly."

No does mean no. The Oregon Ducks, even in their mocking way, were right. But Kinsman says she made it clear, repeatedly, that she did not want to have sex. Winston claims she consented by moaning. Where does that leave us?

Consent should not be this hard to determine, in theory, but it confuses so many. It is also often the point on which these cases turn, be that in the criminal justice system, at the university level, or even on an interpersonal level when a survivor recounts their story. We have such a poor grasp, as a society, on what consent looks like and how it works in practice. This is our collective failure.

In 1998, two Oregon State football players and an eighteen-year-old recruit, along with one other man, were arrested for raping a woman. According to John Canzano at the *Oregonian*, who wrote about the case in November 2014, "There was a search warrant served and evidence logged, including five used condoms retrieved from a bathroom wastebasket, alcohol bottles, and a bag of marijuana. DNA samples were taken, hair and fibers were collected, and clothing was gathered up."[170] The nurse who evaluated the woman told law enforcement, "By all indications this was a case of nonconsensual sex."

The police report says that one of the football players admitted that the woman "told him 'No' repeatedly before and after the oral sex. [He] 'heard her tell the other males "No" when they requested sex acts also.'" The other player told police the entire episode was "a risky situation." According to Canzano, "When asked by police why it was risky, [one player] said, 'I know if she was not saying "No," but you repeatedly ask her to do something and she doesn't want to, you have to be cool.'"

"The suspects," Canzano writes, "told police [the woman] vomited in the restroom, asked to be left alone and said 'No,' at different points of what she described as a seven-hour ordeal."

How could these men continue to have sex with a woman who they admit was throwing up, who wanted to be left alone, and, most damning, said "no" repeatedly?

One answer can be that it was a gang rape and it is easier to continue a given behavior if people you are with are doing it too. One other answer is that we, as a society, have allowed the idea of consent to be murky for so long now that for people who want to violate it, they can excuse away in their minds any evidence that what is happening is nonconsensual. Both of these ideas are terrifying.

In the end, the woman did not want to move forward with the case, and the district attorney said that they did not have one without her testimony. No matter about all the other evidence they had, without the woman taking the stand, the DA's office decided they could not win. This is so troubling considering the fact that people seem to so rarely believe women when they do come forward. Neither option—pressing charges or not—is ideal.

In April 2015, *ProPublica,* in conjunction with the *New Orleans Advocate* and *Sports Illustrated,* published a damning piece about former NFLer Darren Sharper, who has now pleaded guilty to raping nine women in four different states in less than six months.[171] The overall conclusion of the report was that at least part of "Sharper's rampage of druggings and rapes could have been prevented" had law enforcement done their job well at the get-go. But they didn't and that was for two different reasons: 1) people don't trust women when they report, not even the police they are reporting to; and 2) prosecutors feared trying to prosecute such a beloved sports star without an air-tight case (though 1 often makes 2 an impossibility). The piece said, "Studies show that only about one in three victims report sexual assaults in the first place. Of those reports, Department of Justice statistics show, less than 40 percent result in an arrest, a far lower figure than for other major crimes such as murder or aggravated assault." That latter part is due to the fact that "investigations are often cursory, sometimes incompetent, frequently done in ignorance of the suspect's past sex assault history." On top of this, "With police and prosecutors, [victims] found deference toward the accused, and what often felt like disbelief concerning their claims."

So, here we are. Even in examples where police do the legwork and, like at Oregon State, get the people accused of rape to admit that the woman was saying no in addition to a slew of forensic evidence, cases don't move forward if the victim won't take the stand. We demand their eyewitness accounts even as we are prepared to not believe them.

Sexual assault cases are often labeled as "he said/she said," because the central legal question of whether the person reporting the assault gave consent comes down to the two people's accounts. In a society that almost always doubts women and victims in particular, this can be a heavy burden to overcome in a courtroom.

But the Oregon State case seems different. The deputy district attorney told reporters, "The witness has not recanted or changed the statements she originally gave to the police, but without her assistance, the district attorney's office does not have sufficient evidence to file criminal charges." Even when a woman refuses consent and there are witnesses to the crime, the criminal justice system may still fail at its job.

In 2004, at Kansas State, a woman said a player had raped her. The university quickly determined that no criminal act had occurred, despite medical tests having yet to be taken and no word from law enforcement. Less than a week later, prosecutors announced that they were not pressing charges because, according to *USA Today*, "he could not have known the twenty-two-year-old woman who accused him did not consent."[172]

In the case from Colorado in December 2001, the district attorney said in a deposition for a lawsuit against the university, "The recruits had third-party consent that had nothing to do with" the women. "They had been built up by the players to believe that the situation they were going into was specifically to provide them with sex. Their mind-set coming into it was that it was consensual because they had been told it had been set up for that very purpose, and that's what was going to happen."[173]

Neither of these cases shows how consent works. At all. If you don't know if you have consent, then you probably don't. If a person does not feel like they can safely say no, even if asked, there is no consent. And "third-party consent" does not exist; no one else can give consent for another person.

It is not surprising to see this kind of confusion around what consent looks like, though. The concept is often bandied about as if it's some elusive idea that is difficult to understand. This then affects how difficult it is for the public to navigate around these cases with care. Take Jameis Winston as an example. Kinsman told police that she did try to tell him that she didn't consent to what was happening but also that she felt ill and was having trouble talking. Maybe she never actually got out the word "no" or "stop." But that shouldn't matter at all. The burden for establishing consent cannot be on one person alone. Both people need to have an understanding that the other person is giving consent and they need to be sure of it. There is a move to replace "no means no" with consent that is enthusiastically given. "Did you ask her if she wanted to have sex with you and did she say yes?" That is a whole other world from "Did she ever say no or fight back?" If I could choose which world to live in, I'd choose the former. If we taught enthusiastic consent as the acceptable indicator of someone's desire to have sex, then there would be far fewer questions about what happened.

We don't live in that world, though, and so here is the hardest part of all of this for me: Winston may truly believe he did nothing wrong and that he had consensual sex with Kinsman and she may truly believe that he raped her. And so, there is no end to this case for either Winston or Kinsman. Perhaps there may be something of one with the conclusion of their civil suits. More than likely, there will be no tidy wrap-up. The case will forever be a statistic in a sea of such statistics, largely because understandings of consent fail us. We need to fix this.

Voices Against Violence (VAV), a sexual health program at the University of Texas, defines consent as "a YES when it is OK to say NO!"[174] This is an important point: you cannot actually say yes if there is not also space to say no. Consent doesn't exist if anyone is being threatened, coerced, is unconscious, has been drugged, or is unaware (i.e., asleep). So, you need to know 100 percent that your partner(s) is into it and you need to make sure they are able to say no if they need to. VAV has a series of programs to teach the huge university population this message, including posters all around campus with people holding signs with simple messages like, *Unconscious means no,* and, *Silence means no*, and an interactive improvisational program called "Get Sexy. Get Consent." where student-actor facilitators lead students through a series of scenarios in which they can see how consent, boundaries, and communication work in real-time situations.

Universities across the country are creating content like this. But it will be a slow, long process to change how we think, talk, and practice consent.

At the *Harvard Crimson*, Reina A.E. Gattuso wrote beautifully about the many power negotiations that happen in the moments people decide whether or not to consent.[175] She wants to replace the "yes" and the "no" (though she sees and affirms the utility of those two words) with something else. "We make complex decisions, and negotiate, and keep working at it, and don't tolerate coercive bullshit, and do our absolute best," Gattuso writes. "We take responsibility. We try our damnedest to create spaces in which our yeses can echo from the walls, wherein our yeses can motivate angry roommate keep-it-down-in-there texts, wherein 'Am I pretty?' [her code for 'Do you desire/accept me?'] is replaced with 'Am I responsive, am I respectful, am I kind?'"

Rebecca Traister, in a piece for *New York Magazine* that is informed by Gattuso's, writes that sex is messy business and because we often only discuss issues of consent around sexual assault, we flatten the conversation in ways that perpetuate so much of what we are trying to accomplish by having this discussion at all.[176] In the piece, Maya Dusenbery says that her vision for how we talk about sex is not one negatively defined by what sex should not be, but rather, as Traister writes, "a specific vision of what sexual equality could entail." Dusenbery says, "It would include so much more: from the orgasm gap to the truly criminal sexual miseducation of our youth to abortion rights to the sexual double standard. Broadening the scope would not only push us to provide the same kind of deep analysis that's been developed around rape culture in recent years but also help us better see the connections between all the inequities in the sexual culture."

Both Gattuso's and Traister's pieces are important interventions, ones that challenge even what I am writing in this book. We need better education about consent and what it looks like in practice, as well as what its absence looks like. But I agree with Gattuso, Traister, and Dusenbery that there is a much bigger discussion about sex, pleasure, negotiations, and respect that is also necessary.

It cannot just be "no means no," despite how well that works in a postgame taunt. Nor can it simply be "yes means yes," though that's better. What should be taught in locker rooms, health centers, student orientation at universities (or high schools, or middle schools even) is what the University of Georgia's health center says on their "Consent Is Sexy" page: "Consent is a voluntary, sober, imaginative, enthusiastic, creative, wanted, informed, mutual, honest, and verbal agreement."[177] We should all do our absolute best to practice consent this way, in order to be respectful to both ourselves and our partners.

2

PLAY #2
Understand Trauma

There is ample fascination with how people who report traumatic violence change their stories. So much time is spent nitpicking details from different interviews, depositions, and testimonies of the person reporting, and it is pretty common to find inconsistencies. That is a trademark of experiencing trauma.

If we are going to ever have a better conversation about this problem, within college football and beyond, we need a better understanding of how trauma affects the brain. The Jameis Winston case works well for this.

One of the biggest questions around Kinsman's case is the possibility of a drink she had that night being drugged. In the documentary *The Hunting Ground*, which premiered on January 23, 2015 at the Sundance Film Festival, Kinsman says on camera, "I'm fairly certain that there was something in that drink." But two separate tests by the Florida Department of Law Enforcement (FDLE) have shown no evidence of drugs in her system that night. She also went out of her way at the FSU disciplinary hearing to determine if Winston had violated the student code of conduct by assaulting her (they found he did not) to make it clear that she herself never speculated that she had been drugged nor told the police that.

Kinsman's lawyer, John Clune, explained the discrepancy to

me this way: "She knows that the tests did not show the presence of anything, although the tests never keep up with the latest and greatest ways to drug women. For example, at FSU specifically and other college campuses, using Visine as a date rape drug in not uncommon. There are a number of substances that would not show in a test." He went on to tell me, "Erica feels strongly that something was in her drink, but whether she can ever prove it is entirely another matter. She will always believe that there was something in her drink as she did not consume enough alcohol to have the impact she felt after taking that shot."

Once again, we are left with answers that are unsatisfying for everyone.

From the beginning, there have been claims that Kinsman is in this only for the money. This is a common refrain about sexual assault victims, who are often failed by the criminal justice system and so seek some form of justice in the civil courts.

In late September 2014, Winston's attorney, David Cornwell, sent FSU a thirteen-page letter in which he said, according to the *Tampa Bay Times*, that in February 2014, Kinsman's lawyer "demanded $7 million to settle potential claims against FSU, the Tallahassee Police Department, and Winston."[178] But Kinsman's lawyer told the *Tampa Bay Times* that it was Mr. Cornwell who initiated the negotiation over settling. "The facts that Mr. Cornwell chose not to disclose are that it was he himself who reached out to our client's former counsel Patricia Carroll to discuss paying off our client," her attorney told the paper. He also said his client's "main concern was holding Winston accountable, not money, and that Cornwell threatened to sue for civil racketeering." On January 7, 2015, on the same day that Winston announced he would leave FSU and enter the 2015 NFL draft, Kinsman filed a lawsuit against Florida State. Then, on April 16, two weeks before the draft, she filed one against Jameis Winston too. As one commenter on the site *ProFootballTalk* (of all places) put it, "Geniuses, if this were a cash grab, don't you think she'd wait until AFTER the draft to release public information that might negatively effect [sic] his draft stock? It's MENSA up in here."[179]

Perhaps the most popular reason given by people who discount Kinsman's allegations is that she has not had exactly the same recounting of all the events that night, specifically the ones leading up to the moment when she left the bar and got into the cab with Winston and his two teammates. But memories clouded by alcohol and that precede traumatic violence are often unreliable. Rebecca Campbell, a professor of psychology at Michigan State University, gave a presentation at the National Institute for Justice's Research for the Real World Seminar in December 2012, titled "The Neurobiology of Sexual Assault," during which she quoted a fifteen-year police veteran about what it is like to interview sexual assault victims: "The stuff they say makes no sense. So no, I don't always believe them, and yeah, I let them know that. And then they say, 'Never mind. I don't want to do this.' Okay, then. Complainant refused to prosecute; case closed."[180] In the same presentation, Campbell explained that "memory consolidation—it is a slow, fragmented process. It's a documented neurobiological phenomenon" that can be made even worse if the person trying to retrieve and consolidate memories from when they had alcohol in their system. She stressed that "the story may come out as fragmented or sketchy" but "what it really is, most often, is that the victim is having difficulty accessing the memories. Again, the content of the memory the research tell us very clearly is accurate. It's just going to take some time and patience for it to come together." That Kinsman has struggled to piece together those details is as much evidence of her experiencing trauma as it is that she has fabricated events.

All of this must then be contextualized in what we know about false reporting. The very act of reporting sexual assault leads not to questions about how this could happen or who did it but rather if it happened at all. According to the National Center for the Prosecution of Violence Against Women, "The American public dramatically overestimates the percentage of sexual assault reports that are false."[181] Only 2 to 8 percent of rape reports are false. That is on par with all other crimes, except that it is the victims of this particular crime who must constantly prove their trustworthiness before people will even entertain the possibility that they are victims at all.

People also question why Kinsman rode on the back of Winston's scooter afterward, when he drove her back to campus, and why she tweeted nicely about the team and Winston during the 2013 football season before news broke about the case. In the immediate wake of trauma, when someone is unsure of what has just happened or fears repercussions of not going along with the person who has just been violent to them, they will do things that might look confusing on paper. During her 2012 presentation, Campbell said that biologically, many victims respond to violence by releasing hormones, specifically high levels of opiates, that block pain and numb sensation: "The affect that a victim might be communicating during the assault and afterward may be very flat, incredibly monotone—like seeing no emotional reaction, which again sometimes can seem counterintuitive to both the victim and other people." Many victims may also find it difficult to make choices during or immediately follow the trauma, especially if they are still with the person who they feel harmed them. As Campbell put it, "When they're in the middle of the assault, strategies like 'Oh, you coulda, you shoulda, you would have done this'—they can't even think of the options, let alone execute them." We will never understand why Kinsman got on that scooter (she might never understand it either), but it's not evidence that disputes her claims.

All of this combines, so that the way your body reacts to trauma (the release of adrenaline and opiates) in order for your to physically and emotionally survive it is at direct odds with what our legal system demands as far as "proof" of that trauma.

As for what one does months after an assault, there is no script. One of the most famous college sexual assault cases in 2014 was that of Emma Sulkowicz, who carried a fifty-pound mattress around Columbia University "because," she wrote in an op-ed in October 2014, "I want to give visual expression to the struggle that the survivors of sexual violence must endure."[182] Sulkowicz says she was raped in August 2012 by a fellow student, Paul Nungesser, but that the university and the people involved in the disciplinary hearing were hostile toward her. In October 2013, Columbia determined that Nungesser had not raped Sulkowicz. In protest, she said that she would carry the mattress until her rapist was no longer on campus. In February 2015, Cathy Young published a piece at the *Daily Beast* that includes both an interview with Nungesser and Facebook messages between Sulkowicz and Nungesser after the August 2012 incident that were friendly in tone and topic.[183] The latter are included to imply that an assault did not actually happen.

In response to the *Daily Beast* article, an anonymous sexual assault survivor penned a piece for the *Columbia Spectator* in which she wrote, "People react to trauma in unpredictable ways, and one way is to bottle it up, pretend it never happened, and to act like everything's fine. Rape is a terrifying thing to add to your personal narrative—no one wants to think of themselves as a helpless victim . . . For me, I pretended nothing would happen to avoid the social consequences of being the girl who 'cried rape.'"[184] It is unfair to judge Kinsman on what she tweeted months after the night she reported to the police that she had been raped, especially when that behavior aligned with what most of the FSU student body was doing—namely, cheering on the winning football team and its leader.

One part of Kinsman's story that has never changed is crucial when we are talking about the crime itself. Her version of what happened when they got back to Winston's apartment that night has remained consistent since December 7, 2012. The earliest time she told authorities what had happened to her was to an FSU police officer at 3:29 a.m. on December 7, 2012:

> *The next then [sic] she was able to recall was waking up on the floor of someone's apartment. She knew she wasn't at [the bar] Pot Belly's, but she couldn't tell me exactly where she was. The next thing she remembered was being on a bed and a black male having penis to vagina intercourse with her. She stated she saw the door open and another black male with dreads in his hair stand in the doorway while telling the other black male to stop what he was doing. [She] stated she told the black male to stop, but he replied it would be okay . . . She stated she thought the black male took her pants and underwear off and placed them back on after the incident happen [sic]. She was having a hard time remembering what exactly happen [sic] and in what order they happen [sic].*

Just over an hour later, while she was at the hospital being evaluated and having a rape kit done, Kinsman recounted the following to a Tallahassee police officer:

> *Upon arrival at the incident location they went into the*

suspects [sic] room and the suspect removed the victims [sic] clothes and began to have sexual intercourse with her. At some point a person passably [sic] the suspect [sic] roommate entered the room and told the suspect to stop. The victim stated that she was telling the suspect to stop but he did not, she further stated that he [sic] was trying to kick the suspect off of her but was unable to. The suspect also pinned the victims arms down. The suspect then took the victim to the bathroom and continued the assault. She does not remember dressing herself.

Kinsman went to the police the following day and handwrote a statement, in which she said:

We went to an apartment, I don't know where it was. I kept telling him to stop but he took all my clothes off. He started having sex with me and then his roommate came in and told him to stop. He moved us to the bathroom "because the door locked" and I'm not 100 percent sure how everything in there happened. Afterwards I laid on his bed and he put my clothes on . . .

Kinsman once more returned to the police department in February 2013, and gave yet another officer her recollection of that night. He wrote:

She remembers lying on the bed and the suspect taking her clothes off. [She] stated she was "kinda incoherent" and was "just laying there." When he started to have intercourse with her, she stated she told him to stop but wasn't yelling or anything, she was quiet because she felt sick. [She] stated the suspect started out on top of her but then rolled her over

*and tried to put her on top of him but she "just laid there,"
so he rolled her back over. After a little while a male subject
she described as a bigger but not taller (than the suspect)
black male came into the room and told him to stop. The
suspect responded by picking up [Kinsman] and carrying
her to the bathroom. Once in the bathroom, the suspect
told [her] that he could lock that door. He then put her on
the ground and continued the assault. After the assault he
told her that she "could go now."*

At the university disciplinary hearing in December 2014,
Kinsman said:

*I remember being raped on Respondent's [Winston's] bed
clearly. I remember pleading with him to stop clearly. I
remember one of his friends telling him to stop and saying
she is saying no clearly. I remember being carried into the
bathroom and Respondent locking the door behind him. I
remember him holding me down and raping me while I
tried to struggle and resist him. I remember these things as
clearly today as they were in 2012 . . . Respondent raped
me twice on his bed where I lay frozen but telling him to
stop. And again when he put me on the bathroom floor
and locked the door and told me that it was locked. Then
I struggled against him as hard as I could, but he over-
powered me and dragged me. I tried to push and kick him
off of me, but he pinned me down by the arms and leg
like (indicating). I kept telling him to stop, but covered
my face and mouth with one hand and jammed it hard
to the side like this (indicating), like on the floor like this
(indicating).*

The two lawsuits that she filed against FSU and against Winston were the same. In the latter, Kinsman says that Winston took her into his bedroom, removed her clothes, and raped her on the bed despite her protests. While Winston had her on the bed, the suit says, Darby and Casher were watching, with Casher filming part of it. The suit also added a new wrinkle: "Darby also entered the room but told Winston, 'Dude, she is telling you to stop.'" Darby did not say anything about entering the room in either his affidavit or the interview he did with TPD two days later.

The suit goes on to say that after Darby intervened, "Winston picked her up in a fireman's carry, walked her into his bathroom, deposited her onto the hard floor, and locked the door." He then "resumed raping [Kinsman]. She resisted, repeatedly telling him 'no' and 'stop,' and tried to fight him off." He pinned her down, Kinsman says, and covered her "face with a hand and jammed her head to the side" as he continued. When he finished, he picked her "up from the bathroom floor and carried her back to the bed where she lay in shock, unable to dress herself." The suit says he dressed her, told her to leave, and then, when he realized she didn't know where she was, "put her on his scooter" and drove her the false address she gave him.

Much like Campbell described, Kinsman's recounting of the night became clearer the further she was from it, but the basics remained: he undressed her, raped her on the bed before being interrupted, moved her to the bathroom because the door locked, restrained her arms, she struggled, he raped her again, and she said "no" multiple times throughout. At the disciplinary hearing Kinsman said, "Respondent raped me. There is no other term for it. I said it on December 7, 2012, and I'll say it as long as I live because that is what happened."

For some people (probably a lot, possibly most), the very

way trauma works will forever have them doubting Kinsman's version of events. But the fact that trauma works this way needs to be part of how we approach, think about, and talk about sexual violence. Certainly trauma complicates everything, but imagine what it means to the people who experience it. We simply must stop acting like it isn't an important piece of this story; and even though it makes things less clear, this shouldn't be a reason to ignore it.

3

PLAY #3
Go Federal

Title IX coordinators—the people who investigate Title IX cases at universities, including cases where students report that other students have sexually assaulted them—are hired by the universities themselves. Why is that the structure when Title IX is a federal law and university employees have a built-in financial reason to protect the university over and above anything else? It would make more sense for them to be employees of the Department of Education since their job is to make sure the universities are enforcing a federal law correctly. Instead of assuming each institution can train every Title IX coordinator each time one is hired, if they are appointed by the Department of Education and approved by the universities, then their training can be uniform. Also, they would not need to fear being fired by the institution they are keeping an eye on.

If it is possible to get external Title IX coordinators for universities, then maybe it would be possible to get something similar just for athletic departments. Maybe they need their own Title IX coordinators who help establish education and prevention, create rules for responding to allegations and arrests, set up counseling sessions for at-risk players, etc. But they, too, would not be hired or fired by anyone at the university. Not that this serves as a failsafe; people can be intimidated and threatened in ways that don't only involve the stability of their job. It is worth considering, though.

PLAY #4
Intervene, Maybe

Bystander intervention is a tricky concept all around, no matter what experts say about it. The idea is that we will teach everyone to intervene at crucial moments in order to stop sexual violence. By "everyone," I mean everyone who is not the possible perpetrator or victim, but rather people who are on the outside looking in. This is most commonly explained as the person at a party who sees what appears to be a drunk girl being led upstairs by a man. The bystander jumps in, asks the girl if she is okay, maybe even asks her outright if she wants to go upstairs at all, thus giving her the chance to say no and extract herself from a dangerous situation.

Jane Bost is the former associate director of Prevention and Outreach Services at the University of Texas' Counseling and Mental Health Center and she established the Voices Against Violence program, both of which bring attention to the issue of interpersonal violence, promote consent and risk-reduction on campus, and provide services to victims. I interviewed Bost in the spring of 2014 when she was still working at UT and she expanded for me the idea of how bystander intervention works.[185] While many people imagine bystander intervention happening only in the moments before an assault is about to occur, Bost says that it often actually works more indirectly. "It can be, 'You know, that wasn't really a cool way to talk about your girlfriend or boyfriend,'" Bost says. It gives these young people both "a very positive message" and "a sense of empowerment."

All of this is great in theory and as a quick fix to a systemic problem. And so it's incredibly popular on college campuses. If you search the Internet for "bystander intervention," you can easily find guide after guide produced by and for universities on the components of bystander intervention, scenarios when it is useful, and tools for implementing it effectively. President Obama has said, "Bystanders must be taught and emboldened to step in and stop it" when discussing campus sexual assault. He also started the "It's On Us" awareness campaign. On the White House's blog post announcing the campaign in September 2014, it said, "It's On Us asks everyone—men and women across America—to make a personal commitment to step off the sidelines and be part of the solution to campus sexual assault" and then provided a list of things that you can do to be a part of the solution: "Talk to your friends honestly and openly about sexual assault; Don't just be a bystander—if you see something, intervene in any way you can; Trust your gut. If something looks like it might be a bad situation, it probably is; Be direct. Ask someone who looks like they may need help if they're okay; Get someone to help you if you see something— enlist a friend, RA, bartender, or host to help step in," etc.[186]

Michael Winerip told a story in an article for the *New York Times* in February 2014:

> *At a bystander training session for the University of New Hampshire football team last fall, Daniel Rowe, a sophomore, told his teammates that he would use whatever trickery it took to keep them out of trouble.*
>
> *"Maybe you don't get the girl," he said, "but you'll keep your scholarship and still be on the team."*

> *He has watched a drunken teammate pressuring a*
> *woman at a party and pulled him aside. "I said, 'You*
> *know she doesn't want to talk to you, but there's this other*
> *girl downstairs who really likes you.'"*
>
> *There was no girl downstairs.*
>
> *Sometimes, at a big party, Mr. Rowe won't drink,*
> *essentially making himself the designated interventionist.*[187]

This story is amazing, but also terrible. It's great to see a college-aged football player taking this on and caring enough to be actively trying to intervene when he thinks something bad could happen. Yet, he is also deploying tricks because other people around him either don't know enough to understand that they are about to commit sexual assault or they simply don't care. And this is the fundamental issue with treating bystander intervention as an end-all solution: it doesn't actually address the matter of getting perpetrators to, well, stop assaulting people.

There are other concerns as well. In December 2014, Lauren Chief Elk and Shaadi Devereaux penned a piece for the *New Inquiry* titled "The Failure of Bystander Intervention."[188] They note a series of issues with treating bystander intervention as the primary means to prevent sexual assault. First, Chief Elk and Devereaux draw attention to the fact that "there can be serious consequences to physically intervening. Bystanders who 'did what they were supposed to' have ended up injured, incarcerated, or killed." Second, they point out that so much behavior that is technically sexual assault has been normalized in a way that it isn't even obvious to us anymore, leading them to ask, "How can rapists be deterred (or even identified) when no one see [sic] any of these actions as violent to begin with?" Third, they argue that our entire culture is built upon ideas drilled into us beginning in elementary school: ". . . boys are routinely forgiven for ignoring girls' boundaries, children who transgress gender and sexuality norms are targeted for abuse, and school-yard monitors wave away these occurrences with claims of 'boys being boys.'" Fourth, and most devastatingly, they make the real point that when we rely on a system of one-by-one interven-tion, we have to contend with the reality that certain people are considered more worthy of intervening for. "Who is allowed to be a victim and is considered worthy of defense? What happens when the perpetrator of violence has more access to institutions and narratives of humanity than the victim?" Chief Elk and Devereaux ask.

Still, there is one story that indicates what can happen when a football player is the bystander who chooses to intervene.

Rolandis Woodland, a former Mizzou football player, is someone who gives me hope.[189] Missouri swimmer Sasha Menu Courey told multiple people in her life that she had been raped by several Missouri football players in February 2011. It appears she told an athletic staffer a few months later but no investiga-tion was ever done. As I have already discussed, Menu Courey eventually committed suicide. *Outside the Lines* did a report on her case in January 2014.[190] In March 2015, the Columbia, Missouri, police department closed Menu Courey's case, never having identified any of her assailants. Woodland was a football player on the team in 2010 and a friend (and former boyfriend) of Menu Courey. When ESPN showed up at his door, Wood-land chose to talk to them and that alone in the tight-knit world of locker room culture, was a radical act. We need more players to follow in his footsteps.

While at Missouri, Woodland and Menu Courey dated for a short time and remained close friends. Woodland says she contacted him the morning after her assault. "She was dis-traught and crying, confiding to him that something bad had happened to her without saying exactly what," *OTL* reported. Shortly before her death, Woodland says, Menu Courey sent him a video of three of his teammates in a dark room with her. Woodland describes what he saw:

> *You could see her saying, "No, no," hysterically crying . . . She uses the name of [redacted player] when she tells him to get off of her, and he says, "It's only me." They dim the lights and you could see them switching [assaulting] her but you cannot see who was switching because the lights were dimmed. About three minutes into the tape, she pushed whoever was on her off of her and ran out of the room.*

He told *OTL* that following her suicide, he "angrily confronted three of [his teammates]" and that "one of them admitted being with her sexually . . . but denied it was against her consent." That tape is now lost, but Woodland stands by what he saw and what Menu Courey told him.

The *OTL* revelations generated a spike in media coverage, but it was short-lived, with the exception of local reporting in Missouri. Much of the national response focused on explaining away Missouri's culpability or gauging the university's response to the claims, with only a few pieces directly discussing the problem of campus sexual assault. Coverage of the case faded soon after the Columbia Police Department announced they would investigate the case and the University of Missouri Board of Curators agreed to allow an independent counsel to investigate.

Just a few weeks after *Outside the Lines* published the story about Menu Courey, another former Missouri football player, Michael Sam, went to *OTL* to announce that he is gay.[191] Coverage of the story dwarfed the coverage of the rape and death of Menu Courey, with outlets ranging from *ProFootballTalk* to the

New York Times praising the University of Missouri, its football program, the players, and Sam himself. And rightfully so. The university administration, Sam's teammates and coaches, along with students at Missouri had known Sam was gay since August of the previous year. But, according to ESPN, Sam chose to wait on making a bigger announcement until at least the end of the season, and his decision was honored. Once Sam made that announcement, stories appeared with titles like, "Missouri's Campus Celebrates Michael Sam's Announcement," "Mizzou Fraternity Shows Support for Michael Sam," and "Michael Sam Gets Standing Ovation at Missouri Basketball Game."[192] When the NFL draft took place the following May, Sam was one of the most-watched players.

Sam's story—a highly touted NFL prospect announcing he is gay—is a story that fits nicely into a progressive media narrative about ending homophobia in sports. His teammate Woodland's story, on the other hand, speaks to the disturbing pervasiveness of sexual assault on campuses in the US. Sam's story is one in which the locker room at Missouri is a place of acceptance and camaraderie; Woodland's is one in which sexual assault might have been committed by those very same former teammates. In a sports media climate that upholds values that are already understood and respected (say, the tight-knit space of a locker room), Sam is everywhere and Woodland is an after-thought in a story that has become an after-thought.

Today Rolandis Woodland lives in St. Louis and teaches kindergarten, according to *Sports on Earth*'s Gwen Knapp.[193] It was Menu Courey's parents who asked Woodland to speak with *OTL*. They aided *OTL*'s sixteen-month investigation by giving the news team any relevant documents they had. This included Menu Courey's journal where she recorded the assault, a description of her conversation with an athletic department academic advisor in which she disclosed what had happened, and her increasingly distraught feelings.

Woodland told Knapp he made the decision to tell what he knew because "it's too late for Sasha. She can't speak for herself. She needs people to speak for her. I had to do it. She believed in me and I believed in her." He believes her still. Woodland knew, though, that speaking up against his former teammates might hurt people he cares deeply about and could bring him negative attention. "I was scared," he told Knapp. "They're my teammates, and I love those guys . . . They're like my brothers. But this event occurred, and Sasha needed my help."

Perhaps his fear was related to the backlash people often receive when they speak out against football players from high-profile programs. This dynamic was illustrated at Missouri in a different case. A woman reported that a star wide receiver on the football team, while searching for his girlfriend, pushed his way into her friend's apartment and then shoved one of the women who lived there, causing her to fall down at least four stairs. The investigation ended, though, when the woman refused to cooperate with police. A police officer working the case wrote, "She was afraid of the media and community backlash since [the athlete] is a football player for the University of Missouri and is possibly going to be in the NFL draft soon." The officer also wrote that she stated "she was afraid of being harassed and having her property damaged just because she was the victim" and that she "did not want to deal with the mental stress of the whole ordeal—it was already making her physically sick to think about it."

To their credit, the Missouri football staff cut the player from the team because of the incident. (He transferred to Oklahoma and was drafted into the NFL in 2015.) But this fear is unfortunately not misplaced. Many cases of violence against women are referendums on victims and allies, not the perpetrators. When Rolandis Woodland spoke out, for example, Mizzou fans made charges that he was just looking to gain attention. Even so, he told Knapp that none of his teammates had said anything negative to him about his choice.

The *OTL* report seems to have had an effect on the university. In February 2014, the school announced that it had hired an independent counsel "to conduct an investigation to determine whether university employees acted consistent with law and university policy regarding the allegations of the sexual assault or rape of former MU student-athlete Sasha Menu Courey."[194] On April 11, 2014, the Associated Press reported that the independent counsel found that "the University of Missouri failed to follow parts of the federal law that governs sexual harassment on campus."[195] The counsel did not, however, make any recommendations.

The university also launched a task force to assess its policies and procedures for reporting sexual assault. In March 2014, the university newspaper, the *Missourian*, reported that the school was close to revising its confusing employee policy for reporting suspected sexual violence.[196] The article revealed that there was no "mandatory training for MU faculty or staff on how to handle the reporting of Title IX incidents" and that this had led many faculty members to feel unsure of who needs to report or what they need to report. Part of this was resolved by an executive order compelling staff to report sexual assault. (Mandatory reporting, though, can have its own drawbacks, as it makes it impossible for a student to confide in an employee of the university without that case making its way to the disciplinary system.)

And so, while Woodland's choice to speak publicly may not bring legal justice, there is a chance it will help future victims on Missouri's campus. This is no small outcome. At its core, bystander intervention is built around a simple idea: in order to curb sexual assault, victims need allies and advocates, and perpetrators must know that people close to them in their communities will call out their behavior. Woodland is a model for this.

Michael Sam and the community at the University of Missouri, from the administration to the football program to the student body, all deserve recognition for showing what it means to be respectful of how and when a person comes out publicly and for modeling what it means to actively challenge homophobia. But Missouri has another lesson to teach us as well. We should be encouraging more people to be as brave as Rolandis Woodland, to call out sexual assault and be willing to place the safety of others over football. Michael Sam is a hero to many. Rolandis Woodland should be too.

And so, in the end, perhaps we can say that bystander intervention is one idea among many, and despite how often we see it marketed as *the* idea, it is certainly not without flaws.

PLAY #5

Follow the Players

Rolandis Woodland is one football player who did something admirable. He's an example of what one *could* do, not a player actively trying to change the system. But those do exist as well, and if we are going to change the system from the inside, it's worth acknowledging that there are indeed players already doing that.

In 2015, Tyler Perkins was a defensive lineman for the University of Regina in Saskatchewan, Canada, where he helped launch the Man Up Against Violence campaign. He told the CBC that athletes have a particular role to play in helping to end violence against women: "Athletes, especially male athletes, are expected to be the peak of manhood in our society. They are seen as the most manly people and with that comes a lot of expectations. They're expected to womanize and that's very problematic."[197] And Perkins gets that this issue is bigger than physical assault, that it's about a culture that, through silence, continually condones this violent behavior. "Although you might not be doing it yourself—you might not be the one raping someone," Perkins told a local radio station, "but when you don't say something, when you hear these really terrible attitudes about it, then you're allowing other people to do it."[198]

The most famous example of the football player trying to change the locker room discussion about sexual violence is Ohio

State linebacker Jerome Baker. He started talking about this issue in high school. Baker is from Cleveland, not too far from Steubenville, Ohio, site of a now-infamous rape case involving multiple players of a high school's football team. He told ESPN in 2014, "We had the idea to have all the other athletes on the top list in Ohio to sign a pledge to speak out against violence against women."[199] Baker then set up a seminar along with another player, and invited athletes from the area. One hundred and twenty showed up and they discussed domestic violence and sexual assault, and everyone took a public pledge to help end this violence. In 2015, Baker told *SB Nation* he figured out how to utilize his fame for being one of the top football recruits in the county: "'Everyone knew I was being heavily recruited, and would ask if they could work out with me,' Baker says. 'I would say, "Okay, but we're going to talk about this while we work out."' While in the gym, Baker would talk about sexual assault and consent, encouraging his gym mates to join the movement."[200]

Baker continues to encourage people to take the public pledge and to speak out in their own daily lives. In the grand scheme of things, Baker's efforts are small—but ripples always start that way and we have to begin somewhere.

The problem is when someone like Baker runs up against the machine of college football. According to the 2015 *SB Nation* piece, "Baker says he plans to continue his work with sexual assault and violence issues while at Ohio State, but head coach Urban Meyer has yet to agree to allow his players to take the pledge, despite Whoaman's offer. It is unknown why Meyer declined the pledge, or if he has plans for other sexual assault training for his players." That's disappointing, to say the least. But not necessarily surprising. In August 2015, *Bleacher Report* ran a piece about Meyer's "right-hand man," assistant AD for football sports performance, Mickey Marotti.[201] One of the first anecdotes in the piece is a player recounting his first workout with Marotti: "We had to do lunges with weight I could not lift. I looked at him like, 'No, I can't lift it,' and he made me do it, and I'm like falling on the ground. And he's like, 'You p——!' I had never been called a p—— before. For a minute, I thought I was a p——." When your right-hand man that people describe as "the secret weapon for college football's budding dynasty" is calling players "pussies," maybe Baker's message is not one you are willing to listen to.

Baker and Perkins prove that football players can get it. They're a small sampling in the sea of football players, but they give us a glimpse of the possible. The potential for change is there, but someone has to lead. As Marotti's sexist language suggests, relying on coaches has its own problems.

6

PLAY #6
Be Specific

We need universities, and especially teams, to be specific about what preventive education they are doing. It is not enough for Charlie Strong, the head coach at the University of Texas, to simply state that he tells his team one of the core values is "treating women with respect." He got a lot of praise for this and it's good, on its face. But what does that mean? We know it means that if you are arrested for sexual assault you are kicked off the team, which is what happened to two players over the summer of 2014, before Strong had ever stood on the sideline of a game as head coach.[202] Does teaching players to treat women with respect mean that he forthrightly talks to them about consent? Does he ban sexist language?

At Missouri, after those two devastating *Outside the Lines* reports came out in 2014 about multiple football players involved in multiple rapes, head coach Gary Pinkel told the media that Cornell Ford, the cornerbacks coach, "handles that every year in August with our team, he's very specific about rape and no is no, and so on and so forth." Players told the local paper that the coach had given a presentation of somewhere between five and twelve minutes one time during or after practice.

If teams are really in the business of teaching their players to "treat women with respect," then show us what that means. Give us a reason to trust those words by backing them up with concrete education plans. Vague statements are simply not enough anymore.

PLAY #7
Teach Coaches to Teach Boys to Be Men

On October 18, 2014, after the exciting end of FSU's last-minute home win over Notre Dame, Jameis Winston and his head coach, Jimbo Fisher, were surrounded by cameras, personnel, and security. Winston said to Fisher, "Let's enjoy this one right here!" Then Fisher, holding presumably the game ball in his left hand, wrapped his right hand around the back of Winston's gold-sweatband-clad head, pulled the taller player down to his level, and practically stage-whispered into his ear: "Now here's what you've got to do. Calm down, don't give them that overexuberant look. Act very passive right here and get people back on your side. Do you understand what I'm telling you? Humble, humble pie. You got me?"[203]

Fisher choosing that moment to implore Winston to "act very passive," to "calm down," and not to have an "overexuberant look" when speaking to the media in the postgame, is strange. Even more strange is that he made sure to do it publicly, to let us, the media and the fans, know that he, the coach, was giving his player public relations tips. Speaking loudly enough for the microphones and the media standing close by to hear him was not subtle by any means.

This was a major win. It happened a month after Winston had been suspended for lying to FSU athletics about yelling, "Fuck her right in the pussy!" a popular Internet meme at the time, in the school union.[204] It had been just over a week since the *New York Times* published a scathing article critiquing the too-close-for-comfort relationship between FSU athletics and the Tallahassee police department, which implicated Fisher, as the head of the most lucrative and important team in the athletics department, as much as anyone. It also detailed a previously unknown case from November 2012 (a month before Kinsman met Winston), where Winston and Chris Casher, his roommate, were made to lie on the ground and be handcuffed before police determined that they were using BB guns to shoot at squirrels. The *Times* explains: "Later that night, according to the property manager at the nearby Legacy Suites apartments, Mr. Winston, Mr. Casher, Mr. Williams, and another player, Mario Edwards Jr., took part in a shootout that caused $4,200 in damage to thirteen windows." This, on top of what people knew about Kinsman's allegations against Winston, and him stealing crab legs from a grocery store the spring before, is most likely why Winston needed "to get people back on [his] side."

The next day, CBS Sports' Jason La Canfora reported that Winston would probably leave FSU early to enter the NFL draft. (La Canfora was correct, though the public did not find out until January 2015.)

Days later, in Alabama, Fisher could have used his own advice about being humble and passive when talking to the media. In response to being asked if Winston would ever have to face a disciplinary hearing regarding what happened on December 7, 2012 (this was still six weeks before that would happen), Fisher said the team was focusing on the next week's game against Louisville and that "everything should be great."[205] He forced a smile. Then a reporter followed that up with a question about Fisher's reputation and how it had lost its shine amidst all of the issues with Winston. Fisher shook his head and said,

"I don't want to get into this right now. Stop it right now. I'm done." He pulled his mic off his jacket lapel. The reporter responded with, "That's fair," repeatedly. Fisher then gestured to the TV camera, holding his arm out with the palm of his hand up, and asked in an affronted tone, "Now you're going to put this on air?"

But then he did get into it a bit. "Why is my reputation taking a hit?" Fisher asked the reporter. "For backing a kid who has done nothing wrong? I don't want to get into this." He finished by saying he wasn't going to talk about anything else because "the questions [about off-field issues] weren't supposed to be asked today." Then he repeated, "I'm done. I'm done." But after walking away, he turned back to the reporter and questioned whether the video of their exchange would end up on air. I'm not sure if it did. The video is alive and well online, though.

Perhaps recognizing that if the video did hit the air or the Internet, he would seem angry, defensive, or aggressive, Fisher decided to sit down later that day with Solomon Crenshaw of *AL.com*.[206] Fisher told Crenshaw that it was the "school and lawyers" determining everything about the disciplinary hearing, implying he had no say in that process. When asked about the criticism Fisher had received for backing his quarterback, he replied that he did so "by the facts that are out there in the case that is going on. I based my decision based on what are the facts of each situation. If the young man is right, we back him. If he was wrong, he would be disciplined or punished accordingly by whatever is out there. But these are all based on facts of the cases that are out there right now." Shrugging his shoulders, he said, "That's why I stand behind him." He then added, "If the facts change, then we change whatever goes on. But we believe in everything so far, we have no reason not to."

They had no reason not to believe the facts, Fisher said. In truth, they had millions of dollars of reasons to believe the facts that allowed Fisher to keep Winston on the field, which is, most assuredly, the prerogative of a university head football coach. It is his job, even.

That is why I wonder if this man, Jimbo Fisher, is the person we should look to in order to shape football players' character. The coach who waited to give Winston instructions on how to act humbly until they were in front of cameras in the rush of postgame celebrations. The coach who thinks the way to "back this kid" is to not hold him at all accountable for his actions, whatever actions those are (BB gun fights, stolen crab legs, screaming about fucking pussies in public, possibly raping a woman).

Even when Fisher intends to do well, his choices are confusing from the outside. FSU announced in August 2015 that they were going to have a series of speakers to talk to the players about a host of issues including anger management, domestic violence, stress, mental toughness, and sexual assault.[207] First, the list of speakers was only men. Second, the only person on the list who was specifically addressing sexual assault was a man named Adam Ritz. (Ty White was also brought in but his talk is described more broadly than Ritz's.) According to a 2014 local news report out of Eugene, Oregon, Ritz, who had talked to the Oregon football team, was "convicted of sexual battery ten years ago after a woman who babysat his kids accused him of sexual assault."[208] A reporter for the *Ionian* attended one of Ritz's talk in 2011 and she wrote that he frames his own sexual battery accusation as a "bad decision," then "grovels for forgiveness and is pretty much forgiven (evident by the fact that he is hired to speak by colleges across the country)."[209] Who vets these speakers? How do they decide who is talking to these players? Who is in charge?

There is a program that exists already to help coaches who need guidance, though. Futures Without Violence (FWV), which works to end violence against women, children, and families, has created a program called Coaching Boys into Men (CBIM).[210] CBIM started roughly sixteen years ago with "coaching" used as a broad metaphor, the idea being that any man could be a coach to a young man and could positively influence that boy's behavior in his relationships. In 2008, they launched the current version, in which mentoring is actually done by coaches, most of them from high schools (though the program can be scaled to fit a middle school or university program). In short, CBIM is a twelve-week program (which matches the length of a typical high school sport season) during which the coach has or facilitates a fifteen-to-twenty-minute weekly discussion with his team about "respect, integrity, and nonviolence," focusing specifically on dating violence but touching broadly on issues like gender-equitable attitudes. It's designed to invite men to be involved in the work being done to prevent violence—when FWV asks men if they are willing to be active role models in the lives of youth, they get an overwhelmingly positive response.

The program is free (it is available online) and so, according to Brian O'Connor, the director of Public Education Campaigns and Programs for FWV, it's hard to know exactly who is using it and in how many schools it is in, but they do know it's in all fifty states in some capacity. Beyond that, O'Connor says, "We are in about thirty-five to forty communities with an organized implementation," by which he means programs where the coaches are working directly "with our partners on the ground and support." One such example can be found in Arlington, Texas, where Dallas Cowboy Jason Witten's foundation sponsors the program in high schools throughout the area.

It looks like the program does work. According to a randomized controlled trial published in the *Journal of Adolescent Health* in 2012, by the end of the sports season in which a coach did the CBIM program, the players had "statistically significant increases" in their recognition of abusive behaviors and their intentions to intervene if they saw that behavior. CBIM was found to be "one promising strategy to reduce DV perpetration."

Yet, this is just one strategy and its scope is limited. O'Connor says that it works best in cases when the implementation of the program is voluntary, not mandated. A big reason for this is that coaches, like all staff in public education, are strapped for time, and so those who are "on board because they see the value and think [CBIM] is important" are more likely to devote the necessary hours to it. The logic is solid: you don't want men teaching boys about respecting their intimate partners if the coaches are doing it begrudgingly, with resentment, or partially. You can't half-ass equality. At the same time, this means that CBIM is no panacea. What about the boys who might need it the most?

This dovetails with my greatest concern about CBIM and one I addressed with O'Connor: can you really trust *coaches* to educate these boys on this particular topic—the men who are themselves products of the system that CBIM is trying to change? We now live in a post–Jerry Sandusky world where we know that coaches, as much as anyone, can perpetrate dangerous and violent sexual behavior themselves, not to mention encourage (or at least not discourage) the sort of misogyny and homophobia that plagues the language of sports.

O'Connor says that CBIM is oriented toward coaches and players where they are right now in this moment: "These coaches are already in leadership positions and already have influence over these boys, strong influence both positively and negatively." And so, O'Connor says, when he is trying to convince coaches to take up the CBIM mantle, he pointedly tells them that "every day they have a chance to affect these boys."

We need solutions to this intersection of college football and sexual violence. We need them to extend beyond the idea that coaches will impart wisdom and build character. It's not that coaches don't do that—plenty of players will attest that they do—it's just that this is not actually the coach's job, especially not when the stakes are so incredibly high.

PLAY #8
Clean It Up

There are other things that can be done to make a locker room a less sexist and less hostile space. I interviewed Melissa McEwan,[211] creator and editor-in-chief of the feminist site *Shakesville*, who wrote extensively about sexual assault and prevention in the *Atlantic* in September 2013. She told me that "any solution to [the problem of sexual assault] starts with identifying how women are dehumanized within the culture of male collegiate sports, and then taking steps to challenge that dehumanization."

McEwan then provided me a comprehensive list of ideas of how teams can actively challenge that dehumanization:

> *Female students should never, ever be treated by athletic programs as prizes to be handed out to male athletes. Every coach of every male team should start each season by delineating a zero-tolerance policy on sexual assault, which includes information about seeking enthusiastic consent. Every locker room should have a zero-tolerance policy on misogynistic, homophobic, and transphobic language and imagery: No coaches calling the teammates "ladies," and no teammates calling each other "bitch" or "fag." No porn in lockers. Every team should establish a zero-tolerance policy on sexual violence on and off the field, especially as part*

*of team hazing: No slapping each other's asses with towels
in the shower. No forcing the rookies to dress in women's
garments or makeup to earn their stripes.*

Imagine if a team adopted even a portion of these recommendations. McEwan told me that "there is always resistance to these steps, are always complaints that it takes all the 'fun' out of male sports." The reality, she said, is that "this hostile environment already isn't fun for the male athletes who are obliged to affect misogyny to avoid bullying, who have to remain closeted to be safe—and it isn't fun for the victims of male athletes whose predation has been tacitly encouraged by a culture that treats women as a sex class to be consumed." Amen.

PLAY #9
Fire People

If we are ever going to fix what's wrong with college football and sexual violence, we need to start holding the people with power—coaches, athletic directors, university administrators—responsible in meaningful, even punitive ways.

What does it take for an athletic director at a major university to get fired?[212] Colorado State fired their AD in August 2014 because CSU's president had a different vision for the department than did the AD (though it may be because the AD backed the controversial idea of on-campus stadium). Rutgers' AD was all but fired in 2013 after the release of a video showing the university's basketball coach verbally and physically abusing his players. (They had previously fired an AD in 2008 for off-the-books spending and secret deals with the football coach.) In 2012, Montana fired theirs (along with their head football coach) after a series of sexual assaults and gang rapes committed by players came to light and prompted federal investigations into the department. That same year, Tulsa fired their AD for betting on football games. Georgia's AD was asked to resign after he was arrested for DUI. In 2003, Kansas fired their AD supposedly because then–basketball head coach Roy Williams didn't like him.

Maybe we should be firing more. How many players have to be accused, arrested, or convicted before your job is jeopardized?

There are people at the university who are actively failing to put into place preventive education, to teach consent, to respond when cases come through, and sometimes to purposefully minimize them in order to keep players on the field. Those people's feet, though, are so rarely held to the fire. The system is set up to push all responsibility onto the individual players even though it's possible to identify visible patterns of how universities handle these cases.

The higher-ups at universities need to be held accountable for failing victims and protecting players, especially once established patterns emerge of different players committing violence under that university president or athletic director or coach. Either figure out how to support players better and actively work to change the culture on your team, or you're done.

PLAY #10
Do Anything

The NCAA should just do something, anything, at this point, beyond empty words and publishing PDFs that programs might look at.

There are steps that the NCAA can take to make the culture surrounding D1 sports less dangerous for women. Heather Corinna, a sexuality activist and founder of *Scarleteen*, a site dedicated to providing sex education and resources to young adults, says, "If we want to keep making progress reducing—and, hopefully, eventually eradicating—sexual abuse and assault," we need to educate people to "understand that sex or women aren't things to take."[213] Which means that first, the association should revisit and revise its rules on what can and can't be offered to athletic prospects in recruiting.

One action the NCAA could take to prevent future cases like this one is to put explicit language in their bylaws that says that student hosts are not allowed to have sex with potential student-athletes during the recruitment process. Undoubtedly there are cases where recruits and hostesses are both consenting partners (this is probably the vast majority of them), but those do not mitigate the larger issues that arise from failing to prevent sex between people in these two groups and the message that conveys to the players.

And the NCAA has the jurisdiction to prohibit it; it already limits how many schools recruits can visit, how long their visits can last, who can talk to them (and for how long), and what kind of events they can attend. Another fact to take into consideration is that sex between seventeen-year-old recruits and older university students might actually break age-of-consent laws, depending on where the school is located. Taking an active and clear position against sexual activities between recruits and student hosts, then, would limit the legal risks for the university and their students. It would also show that the NCAA is committed to helping end practices that place women in particularly vulnerable positions.

On a more innocuous level, the NCAA could outright ban programs using the images of women to recruit players. "Hey College Coaches, Stop Recruiting with Creepy Female Celebrity Photoshops" is an actual headline of a post at *SB Nation*, from April 2015.[214] The image that inspired the post was tweeted by the tight ends coach for the University of Pittsburgh. It is the 2015 cover of *Sports Illustrated* with the model's bathing suit photoshopped to the blue and yellow of Pitt's colors, the word *Pitt* running across the left breast of her bikini. In the photo, the model appears to be removing the bottom of her suit and she is at that critical moment just before revealing her most private of areas. The coach deleted the tweet within minutes.

In August 2014, a recruit, Shy Tuttle, tweeted a photoshopped cover of *Rolling Stone* that featured a picture of himself next to Beyoncé. Someone from the University of Tennessee had supposedly created this as a humorous enticement to Tuttle. The image even included custom article teasers: "Beyoncé on why she thinks Tuttle belongs at Tennessee." Tuttle chose Tennessee. Wake Forest did something similar with Kim Kardashian and Selena Gomez.

To be fair, these schools will also photoshop these men as

gladiators or superheroes, though women are too often portrayed as accessories available to them. These are high school boys getting these images as part of their recruitment. We need to seriously consider why teams feel this is effective messaging.

More radically, the NCAA could call for the end of hostess programs altogether. That would take the burden off the actions of individual hosts and instead place the responsibility on the athletic programs themselves. The NCAA should suggest alternative programs that schools can implement to allow nonathletes to continue their active support of the athletics department.

The NCAA also needs to acknowledge the impact that its ban on financial compensation to players has on the way hostess programs are used by athletic departments. In September 2013 and June 2014, the president of the NCAA said that he still believes firmly that student-athletes should not be financially compensated.[215] But for the last fifty years, certain NCAA schools have been using beautiful, kind hostesses as an example of what that recruit will gain by attending that particular university. These women are a stand-in for the financial compensation that the NCAA denies players. Many people have called for college athletes to get paid. One reason to add to the list is that it would reduce the pressure on programs to use women as a substitute.

And finally, the NCAA needs to move beyond simply offering to host educational sessions and national summits on sexual assault prevention. It should also spend its resources actually enforcing rules and levying sanctions on programs where players continue this harmful behavior and where other players, staff members, or coaches cover it up.

Jill Gaulding, a former faculty member at the University of Iowa College of Law and cofounder of Gender Justice, a nonprofit law firm that eliminates gender barriers, said, "When it wants to, the NCAA puts real teeth into its enforcement."[216] "The NCAA has explicit principles that relate to gender equity and nondiscrimination," Gaulding told me. Those principles "state that the NCAA shall 'promote an atmosphere of respect and sensitivity to the dignity of every person.'" It is these principles under which the NCAA claimed authority to punish Penn State's football program following the Jerry Sandusky conspiracy. In ignoring the way that their own policies lead to football programs using women as lures for recruits and by turning their backs on sexual assault committed by players, the NCAA is failing to promote that atmosphere of respect and dignity.

Gaulding says these kinds of changes are necessary because "for faculty and students at the school, the harm is direct—it creates a hostile environment that impinges on their ability to teach or learn." For those not directly affected by the use of hostess groups or the NCAA often failing to acknowledge the problem of sexual assault, "the harm is indirect, but nonetheless real. Our brains soak up messages about gender roles and the relative value of men and women. Every biased message we soak up makes us that much more likely to discriminate on the basis of gender."

Gaulding summed it up this way: "When it wants to, the NCAA puts real teeth into its enforcement."

As Corinna says, sports is an area that many consider "the most masculine of places." If the culture in football programs can be changed, even in small, incremental doses, to better respect the humanity of women, the effect of those changes will extend far beyond the perimeters of these campuses.

PLAY #11
Do Better

Sports media just need to do a better job with how they report on this topic. It's that simple. I asked a handful of experts what they recommend.[217]

"Women who are sexual assault victims need to be treated like human beings," and sports journalists need to "talk about [the problem] and stop pretending like it isn't there," says Dave Zirin, the sports editor at the *Nation*. Zirin writes extensively on the intersection of sports and culture. In November 2010, he argued that the Notre Dame football program needed to be shut down after the death of Lizzy Seeberg.[218] "Seeberg overdosed," Zirin wrote, "on antidepressants ten days after telling friends and campus police that a University of Notre Dame football player had sexually assaulted her." Zirin went on to explain how the team reacted:

> It's a horrible story that shines light on something that occurs on far too many campuses, where sexual assault is part of the culture of entitlement conjoined with big-time men's college athletics. But even worse was the response by the supposed adults in charge. Less than a month after the death of Declan Sullivan, Coach Brian Kelly—the guy with all that "character," remember—was asked by reporters about Seeberg's suicide. Coach Kelly repeatedly deflected

the question. When the fourth reporter from the Tribune Company asked Coach Kelly, he smirked, "I didn't know you guys could afford all those guys," referring to the financial foibles at the paper.

Zirin says it is embarrassing how basic his advice is for other sports journalists, but that it is necessary because there's this "assumption that many sports writers have that there is this line of women looking to trap athletes in sexual assault allegations." He says this "is not only untrue but I think reflects more the fantasy of overwhelmingly male writers who write about sports, as opposed to the reality. Unfortunately, the reality is far more that to be a big-time athlete is to live in a world of entitlement and for many big-time athletes that entitlement extends into violence against women, and many members of the media, I would argue, enable that entitlement" by portraying athletes as "macho supergods" and potential victims as opportunistic. Reporters need to "stop speaking about women who are brave enough to come forward as if they absolutely, positively must have an agenda that is rooted in somehow a financial motivation or trapping of an unsuspecting male superstar."

This idea that sexual assault is not a serious problem then bleeds into other sports reporting, specifically how issues of violence against women rapidly leave the radar and are rarely questioned. "For example," Zirin says, "Jovan Belcher took his own life the month before the NFL playoffs when Roger Goodell [the commissioner of the NFL] does his round of interviews and no one in media asks him about the issue of violence against women." For Zirin, this is a "little thing" with a big impact because it maintains a silence around the issue that allows it to go unchecked.

Julie DiCaro, founder and CEO of *Aerys Sports*, and a former attorney, warns journalists that you can never "assume that you know anyone," even if you have a relationship with them through years of reporting. She also says that people in the media need to stop speculating on whether a rape has taken place based on what the accuser does following the assault. "Don't assume that you know how a victim is going to act," DiCaro says. "Everybody reacts differently and for some women, it takes time for them to understand, 'That's what happened to me.' For me, for weeks, days, and months, I was like, 'I put myself in the situation. I was drinking. I left a party with the guy. Would you really call it rape?' It wasn't until much later that I was like, 'It was rape. I couldn't get him to stop. I was trying to push him off me. I kept telling him "no." He did it anyway. That's rape.'"

DiCaro wrote about being sexually assaulted in December 2013 for *Deadspin* in a piece titled "Why I Believe Jameis Winston's Accuser."[219] In her piece she details her own rape and why she never reported it. DiCaro wrote:

> *I'm no shrinking violet, and those who now know about my rape are surprised that I didn't stand up for myself, that I didn't scream bloody murder from the rooftops about what happened to me. The only explanation I have is that I was one girl, a very young girl, and I believed that I would be up against several adult male police officers. It never occurred to me that I might tell them my story and they would believe me. From the beginning, my assumption was that they would side with my rapist, and it would be my job to convince them otherwise. I suppose I believed this because of the way I'd seen rape victims treated in the media.*

From her experience as a lawyer, DiCaro says that journalists need to "get a copy of the police report and read it, if you can. That's where the police start building their case, where you are going to start seeing evidence in the case." She also says that there just needs to be a better understanding of "what the threshold is for indicting someone or finding someone guilty in criminal court. In this era of *CSI*, 'Well, there's no witnesses—if you don't have pictures, it didn't happen.'" But that distorts the reality of what happens in a courtroom and what is asked of the juries by the legal system. DiCaro notes that the burden of proof in a criminal case is not that you must prove 100 percent that someone committed a crime. Instead, "the standard is 'beyond a reasonable doubt,' which means reasonable people would be, 'Yeah, he did it.'"

Melissa McEwan, founder and editor-in-chief of the site *Shakesville*, who has written hundreds of pieces about the impact of rape culture on our larger society, echoes DiCaro's point about journalists being more honest about how the criminal justice system works. McEwan says that an essential part of writing fairly about these cases is first "familiarizing yourself with rape statistics, especially around false reporting." Most specifically, she states that "the lack of a conviction is not the same thing as a false report," though the two are often conflated. As McEwan explains, "A lot of sexual violence and domestic violence does not ever get reported and the incidents that do get reported, a lot of those do not result in any kind of charges and even fewer in prosecution and even fewer in conviction. Of the many, many, many cases of sexual violence and domestic violence, very few of them result in convictions."

Dr. David J. Leonard, associate professor and chair of the the Department of Critical Culture, Gender, and Race Studies at Washington State University, cautions about assumptions in either direction: "Don't mistake a lack of a trial or conviction as exoneration. Differentiate between the decisions of the criminal justice system, plagued by misogyny, sexism, racism, and countless other ideologies that are antithetical to justice and discussion of justice, fairness, and combating issues of domestic violence." He goes on, "At the same time, don't take an arrest or an accusation as a conviction."

In addition to being more familiar with statistics about false reporting, McEwan says that for someone to write responsibly on the topic of sexual assault, they must "familiarize themselves with rape culture narratives to ensure that they are not upholding them." McEwan wrote an essay in 2009 titled "Rape Culture 101" that is one of the best pieces to explain these narratives in detail.[220] It is difficult to quote the essay because it is a long, comprehensive list of many different examples from our culture of how rape is minimized, ignored, sanitized, and even sanctioned (implicitly and explicitly). One example is:

> Rape culture is refusing to acknowledge that the only thing that the victim of every rapist shares in common is bad fucking luck. Rape culture is refusing to acknowledge that the only thing a person can do to avoid being raped is never be in the same room as a rapist. Rape culture is avoiding talking about what an absurdly unreasonable expectation that is, since rapists don't announce themselves or wear signs or glow purple.

McEwan says that "if you are familiar with [rape culture narratives], then you can avoid the pitfall [of using them] in the first place." She also implores journalists to be empathetic when imagining what it is like in a climate hostile to sexual assault victims to report a crime, especially to report "sexual violence against a prominent person." It is "not just the legal hoops," she argues, "but also the emotional calculations that people make when they are reporting sexual violence." Not only is your body scrutinized but so is your sexual history. Every action made by an alleged sexual assault victim both before and after the assault is put under a microscope and picked apart. They are often vilified, all while there being a very low chance for conviction. "If people understand what the personal costs of reporting sexual violence really are," McEwan says, "they would be less likely to make implications or outright say someone is a gold digger or say someone is doing it for fame and fortune, that someone is doing it to just punish someone. If you really understand the personal costs, you are not inclined to make that judgment."

Leonard often writes about the intersection of sports and race. Following the murder-suicide of Jovan Belcher, he published a piece at the *Feminist Wire* titled, "Kasandra Michelle Perkins: We Must Say Her Name."[221] Leonard wrote:

> *While there are clearly issues specific to football—impact of concussions, the culture of hypermasculinity, mental health—we cannot lose focus on Kasandra Michelle Perkins. Her life is no less precious just because she didn't play linebacker; her life is no less important because she didn't have teammates (although her family and friends are her teammates) grieving. Her story is no less important because we live in a culture that privileges football and celebrity over the daily tragedies of violence.*

In thinking about the overlap of sports, race, and gender in relation to reporting on sexual assault, Leonard notes that "there is a tendency to chronicle each incident, each report, in sensationalistic terms that play on stereotypes of athletes, particularly black athletes." We must give each story care and provide it with its appropriate context.

Sports journalists need to be more aware of the assumptions that cloud how reporters think about sexual assault victims and how they write about these cases. How the media address sexual assault has an impact on society at large because it is within sports media that we often talk about this particular issue.

For, as Leonard suggests, failure to treat each story with the care it deserves means that journalists "contribute to stereotypes and a flattened understanding of the violence," and "it erases the victims, it erases the culture of violence, and it erases the daily harm."

12

PLAY #12
Calm Down

Fans need to calm down. And get some empathy. But mainly, calm down.

If you have never been on the wrong side of a discussion with a fandom over the troubling off-field behavior of one of their players, count yourself lucky. It's an intense experience. College football fans, especially in these days of social media, can be an aggressive bunch, especially if they feel their team has been attacked in some way. In an August 2015 piece at the *Kernel* about "Why #FSUTwitter Is Football's Most Feared Digital Mob," Dan Wolken, a *USA Today* sports writer, talked about his experience with FSU fans after the media started to cover the Winston rape investigation.[222] "The way it all unfolded fed into a lot of the defensiveness, the clannishness, and the anti-media sentiment," Wolken told the Kernel. "They were able to craft this narrative that the people who were writing this stuff were people who had it out for Florida State. Which is, of course, ridiculous. But when you want to believe that you're being attacked, you can take anything written about Florida State and say it's evidence that you're being attacked. That's not the way that most people working in the media would see it." The media think they are doing their job; fans see anything that can be construed negatively on their team as an attack by that media. It's a hard circle to get out of when a case like Winston's is unfolding.

The NCAA actually has a page dedicated to explaining sports fandom and why people get so attached to a team.[223] It reads, "A recent survey concluded that being identified with their favorite team is more important to people than being identified with their work and social groups, and as important to them as being identified with their religion." And then explains the extreme to which fans will go: "Highly identified sports fans are passionate: they would consider doing a number of extreme behaviors, including aggressive actions, outrageous deeds (e.g., give up sweets for a year, destroy a favorite keepsake), and engaging in superstitious rituals (e.g., wearing lucky clothing, sitting in a lucky seat) if the action improved or guaranteed their team a championship or victory." The page then lists the psychological benefits of being a fan, including support from other fans, companionship, lower stress, and a sense of belonging.

According to Eric Simons, author of *The Secret Lives of Sports Fans: The Science of Sports Obsession*, who wrote a piece about sports fandom for the *Washington Post* in January 2015, "A sports team is an expression of a fan's sense of self . . . In all kinds of unconscious ways, a fan mirrors the feelings, actions, and even hormones of the players. Self-esteem rides on the outcome of the game and the image of the franchise."[224] It is this latter aspect of being a fan—your own self-esteem being attached to a game or the reputation of your team—that makes some people react so nastily to media that they feel are hostile to their team. Then couple that with discussions of sexual violence, a topic that is heated and disputed no matter what area of life is being discussed.

We are talking not just of fan identity here, which Simons says can be all-encompassing: "Athletic teams offer not just a connection with the players and fellow fans, but also with regional pride, family relationships, color preferences, aesthetic tastes, and even moral standards. Teams or players can assume religious, ethnic, or political identities." When we talk about sexual violence in conjunction with one's favorite team, the love of team is bolstered by endless cultural narratives that paint victims as liars, gold diggers, and opportunists. The anger that fans have for the media who report on this topic is even more charged when directed at the people who report players for violent behavior. This is why it is so common to hear women say they did not report because of their fear of the backlash from the university community and fans.

Fans need to calm down.

13

PLAY #13
Hire Women

In 2013, the Institute for Diversity and Ethics in Sport released a report card that assessed the hiring practices of "over 150 newspapers and websites" on their racial and gender hiring practices.[225] For the third report in a row, gender hiring practices received a resounding "F." The numbers from the report are jaw-dropping: "This report shows that in 2012, 90.9 percent of the sports editors, 86.6 percent of the assistant sports editors, 83.9 percent of our columnists, 86.3 percent of our reporters, and 86 percent of our copy editors/designers were white. The percentages of males in those positions this year are 90.4, 82.8, 90.2, 88.3, and 80.4." Other highlights from the report included no Latina or female Asian sports columnists at all; of the thirty-five women who were columnists, only two were African American (Shannon Owens and Jemele Hill); and 11.7 percent of all sports reporters were women. This is an important issue because the sport itself is so racialized in terms of who holds the power (university presidents, athletic directors, coaches, the NCAA administration, and the sports media) versus who does the labor on the field and gets scrutinized for off-field troubles (mainly black men). Sports media need a much wider range of diversity to make sure this issue is covered fairly.

The Women's Media Center found similar problems within the field of sports journalism. Their 2014 report on "The Status of Women in the US Media," stated that "The bleakest of realities show that those who steer sports news coverage remain overwhelmingly white and male, even as women's sports and the ranks of sports fans who happen to be women are surging."[226] This was true across all sports media. Of the 183 sports talk radio hosts, only two were women and they "either were paired or tripled with male commentators," the report notes.

What this means is that when it comes time for sports media to cover issues of sexual assault or violence against women in any form, they turn to their huge cast of men to talk about a crime whose victims are overwhelmingly women. And since we are talking about football in particular, it is a lot of white men talking about a crime whose victims are very likely to be black women (since black men are overrepresented at all levels of football as compared to the general population). And they are talking about all of this while focusing primarily on the alleged perpetrators—the athletes—which makes the athletes the protagonists in stories where they are harming others.

Inevitably, then, victims of sexual assault are often painted as liars, opportunists, confused, revengeful, or regretful after consensual sex. This same dynamic exists in most of our culture, including media, law enforcement, and the legal system. And the outcome of this kind of narrative feeds into a culture where many survivors never report their assaults and feel that they are at fault for a crime committed against them. Of course, there are people who falsely report, but those numbers are extremely small because women who report are so rarely believed and their private sexual lives are often put on trial in the public sphere. Since this is the case, sports journalists have a special responsibility to be fair in how they write about sexual assault cases.

And it's not like this is impossible to accomplish. An easy fix is to just have more women offering commentary in sports media. On September 30, 2014, CBS Sports Network debuted *We Need to Talk*, a horribly named show that had a stellar premise: allow a diverse women-only cast to talk about sports for an hour on a weekly basis.[227] They opened the show by addressing what was then the biggest ongoing sports story: multiple NFL players accused of or arrested for domestic violence, including former Ravens running back Ray Rice and Vikings running back Adrian Peterson, among others. About twenty minutes in, veteran sports journalist Dana Jacobson led a discussion on what all of this coverage meant to victims of domestic violence, which was a rarity among the countless hours devoted to the topic across sports media in the previous month. Sitting on the couch with Jacobson were Lisa Leslie and Swin Cash, former WNBA stars and Olympic medalists, and Dara Torres, an Olympic swimming champion. And all three of these women announced that they had been either physically or emotionally abused in past relationships. Here's the hard truth about all of this: if you get a few women in a room, the odds are high that among them will be a victim of violence at the hands of a partner and/or sexual assault.

The discussion was intense. Swin Cash talked about dealing with her own violence privately and she wondered aloud about Ray Rice's wife and the impact of the coverage on her life. Leslie challenged that all women should up and leave the first time violence happens in their relationship, but Cash countered, noting that much of the abuse is psychological. That prompted Torres to explain that it took her a long time to realize that she had been in an abusive relationship because it was emotional, not physical. Finally, Cash just went in on the powers-that-be, saying, "Not just the players—the owners, administrators, agents . . . everyone that is making money off of the NFL needs to be held accountable for domestic violence. If they start there, everyone else will fall in line because they have that much power." To have such words be said by a survivor in a conversation about victims (instead of the normal one that focuses on the perpetrators) was a powerful and important moment in what had otherwise been a rather homogenous discussion. And it was offered to us because a diverse group of women were given the space to have that discussion within sports media.

We need more spaces like that—we need them on big platforms, and we need them consistently.

And as much as we need more women in sports media, we need them in locker rooms too. We need teams to hire women in all kinds of roles. We need gender, sex, and sexual orientation diversity in the athletics generally, football specifically, if ever we are going to force these players and their coaches and even their athletic directors to take the humanity of women (and any potential victims) seriously.

At the same time, Donald McPherson, a social justice activist and former NFL quarterback, says that we need leadership on this issue from men—"for men to give other men permission to move beyond gendered roles in society. To say, 'You can play football and be a loving, caring, empathetic person off the field.'"[228]

If we can one day get football and empathy in the same conversations on a regular basis, we will have a sure sign that we are doing something right.

CONCLUSION
Change Is Possible

On August 5, 2015, sitting in my office in Austin, Texas, I got a specific tip from a source whom I trust a lot. They gave me the name of a Baylor football player, Samuel Ukwuachu, and told me he was about to go to trial for sexually assaulting a fellow student. After hanging up the phone, I searched "Ukwuachu" on the Internet, along with every word I could think of that would give me even a brief blotter mention of an arrest, indictment, or trial date for a sexual assault charge. I couldn't locate anything. That's when I contacted my friend Dan Solomon, a writer at large for *Texas Monthly*, and asked for his help. Within minutes, Dan had located Ukwuachu's name on a trial docket, which Dan forwarded to me. After looking the document over, I realized Ukwauchu was only twelve days from trial. Less than an hour later, Dan and I were in the car and on our way to Waco, a small town in central Texas located about an hour and a half north of Austin. In the center of Waco sits the Baylor campus. During the ride, we speculated endlessly about how it was that a player at a football team then ranked in the top four nationally could almost make it to trial for a violent crime in a small town and there be no word of it anywhere.

Turns out, that same day, as we were driving back to Austin after looking at the case file, the *Waco Tribune* broke the story. For whatever reason, that report was a blip on the media radar and almost no other outlet picked it up. Over the next fifteen days, Dan and I worked on the story relentlessly. I am a great researcher and gatherer of facts, while Dan is a magnificent storyteller with an eye for what is necessary to report in the most effective and clearest manner. We pored over the documents we had, talked to sources, crafted a narrative, and argued about what had to make it in and what didn't. We attended the first two days of the trial in Waco. We wrote and brainstormed during the three-hour-round-trip car rides and during late-night texting and Google Drive sessions. In just over two weeks, we went from receiving the tip to publishing our piece at *Texas Monthly*. The story, "Silence at Baylor," ran on the morning of August 20, 2015, as testimony was still being presented in the courtroom.[229]

We chronicled how Ukwuachu, who was a freshmen all-American defensive end, left Boise State in 2013 after his first year. His dismissal followed a violent episode where Ukwuachu hurt himself. People on the football staff feared for Ukwuachu's girlfriend's and his roommate's safety. Ukwuachu then transferred to Baylor but did not receive a waiver from the NCAA, so was ineligible to play his first year in Waco and had to sit out the 2013 season. Within months of arriving on campus, in October 2013, a female soccer player reported to both the Waco Police Department and the university that Ukwuachu had raped her. Neither the police nor the school did much with it. The university, after a cursory investigation, determined that Ukwuachu did not violate their student code of conduct. The Waco PD eventually suspended the case. Then in the spring, the Waco PD handed the case over to the county DA, who took it to a grand jury. The grand jury issued an indictment for two counts of sexual assault against Ukwuachu in June 2014.

When Baylor announced that Ukwuachu would miss the

2014 season for "some issues," no one looked into what those issues could be and certainly it was never reported that they were
in fact felony assault charges pending trial. Ukwuachu remained
on a football scholarship, attended classes, and eventually graduated. The woman who reported him, though, had left campus
at the end of the spring 2014 semester. She had injured herself
in the summer of 2013 and was rehabbing her leg that fall. After
the assault, due to the effects of her post-traumatic stress disorder
(PTSD), she was unable to do as much rehabilitation as she needed
to, her scholarship was reduced, and she had to leave Baylor.

In the summer of 2015, weeks before Ukwuachu was about
to go to trial, Baylor's defensive coordinator, Phil Bennett, announced that he expected Ukwuachu back on the field soon.
Bennett did not mention anything about the charges or the
possibility that his player could be found guilty of them. In the
end, Bennett was wrong.

Ukwuachu was found guilty that August and sentenced to
180 days in county jail, ten years probation, and 400 hours of
community service. He appealed the case to the Texas Supreme
Court and was released from jail pending the appeal.

The story Dan and I reported about this case blew up into
a national story that led the sports news cycle for about a week.
The head coach of Baylor, Art Briles, defended his acceptance
of Ukwuachu's transfer and keeping him on the team after the
reported rape. The local media defended themselves against the
fact that they had never reported on the case until just before
the trial. The university defended itself against charges that it
did not do enough to protect the woman or other women on
campus.

Baylor launched an internal investigation and then hired an
outside firm to do one. Their goal is to identify weaknesses in their
policies regarding sexual assault reporting and what failed in this

particular case. In late 2015, the woman's attorney announced that she had settled with the university; no details of the settlement were released to the public.

The week after our piece ran, the Big 12 athletic directors met to discuss and adopt conference-wide rules. During that meeting, they talked about the news out of Waco and decided to adopt a new transfer rule, one in the style of a rule the SEC had enacted earlier that year. It declared that any member institution would no longer be allowed to accept the transfer of a student-athlete who had been released from their former team for serious misconduct, including sexual and/or domestic violence.

This is not a catchall solution and is only a small step. As we know, teams are good at not knowing what they don't need to in order to skirt the rules and remain innocent of wrongdoing—that could happen with this transfer rule and most likely will. But the SEC and the Big 12, two of the biggest college football conferences in the country, within months of each other, adopting a transfer rule like this shows that universities recognized that their old "Nothing to See Here" plays are not nearly as effective as they once were.

The best evidence of this is Baylor itself. In May 2016, Pepper Hamilton—the law firm doing the external investigation into how Baylor had handled reports of sexual violence—completed their work and briefed the university's board of regents. The board then decided, due to the extent of the problems uncovered, that they would fire the head coach, Art Briles, demote the president of the university, Ken Starr, to chancellor and law professor, and put the athletic director, Ian McCaw, on probation.

Briles had to go due to the law firm's findings, which expressed "significant concerns about the tone and culture within Baylor's football program as it relates to accountability for all forms of athlete misconduct." More specifically, Pepper Hamil-ton discovered, according to the Findings of Fact released by the university, that the "football program and athletics department leadership" had failed "to identify and respond to a pattern of sexual violence by a football player, to take action in response to reports of a sexual assault by multiple football players, and to take action in response to a report of dating violence."

On May 30, Baylor announced that they had hired Jim Grobe to come in as interim head coach. McCaw then imme-diately resigned, saying in a statement, "I have decided that a change in athletics department leadership is in Baylor Universi-ty's best interest in order to promote the unity, healing, and res-toration that must occur in order to move forward." Two days later, on June 1, Starr stepped down as chancellor, saying he was doing so "as a matter of conscience." He retained his position in the university's law school.

Briles's firing is momentous in the history of college football and sexual assault. Baylor was a top-ranked national champion-ship contender under him, the university completed the con-struction of a $266 million stadium in August 2014, and Briles was under contract with the university until 2023. Interrupt-ing his tenure in this way and at that time was unprecedented. Montana's Robin Pflugrad and Colorado's Gary Barnett are the closest parallels, but neither was coaching as promising a team as Briles was. Pflugrad was let go in 2012 when his contract ended, and Barnett continued to coach following several scan-dals, only being forced out—with a $3 million buyout—after a disappointing 2005 season on the field. Briles got no extra time and no soft landing. He was held accountable for the failures of a system he oversaw. Perhaps this was a watershed moment in the sport. We shall see.

The SEC and the Big 12, and Baylor in particular, are forging new plays because we are forcing them to, and for once that means considering consequences that rewrite the order of things, putting potential victims above winning on the field. Creating new plays for the playbook is possible, even if it is slow.

On a personal level, as a fan of the sport and an advocate for reducing and ending sexual violence, I need those new plays and I need them *now*. I need to know that the sport I love sees sexual assault and rape as unsportsmanlike conduct, as fundamentally opposite to the spirit of the game.

I say this because I am not a person who can operate in some neutral space where I put aside what I know about these programs, the NCAA, the media, and intense college football fandom.

In January 2014, my team—Florida State—won the national championship, and Jameis Winston, our quarterback who had very recently not been charged with sexual assault, won the award for "most valuable player" for last-minute heroics in the game. The team went on to remain at the top of the polls the next season and played in the first-ever college football playoffs. (They lost in the semifinals to Oregon.) Despite all of my personal objections and my own acknowledgment that by watching I am participating in the very system I spend my life critiquing, I've watched nearly every game over the last few seasons, having hoped that they'd win but also that they'd lose and that if they did, I could possibly stop caring so much. The great, lifelong hold that FSU football has on my heart has struggled with what I questioned about the quarterback who led the team onto the field and about the university, my alma mater, that he represented.

There will be people who think I should, somehow, be able to turn off my brain or compartmentalize my knowledge. I simply cannot, though a part of me wishes I could watch the game detached from all of this. The FSU fan in me is desperate to feel the high of cheering on my team without the weight of knowing the cost of the system that creates football champions. I think back to my 1999–2000 self, a student who paid little attention to the details of off-field problems and focused on the game itself. Ignorance, as they say, is bliss.

I bleed garnet and gold, but that blood now flows into a brain that is no longer ignorant, nor blissful. And all of it together makes my heart hurt.

It's time to do something about that.

ENDNOTES

Introduction

1 Tom Friend, "Justice Is Served," *ESPN the Magazine*, December 6, 2001.

2 Matt Baker, "FSU's Winston Investigated in Sexual Assault Complaint," *Tampa Bay Times*, November 13, 2013, http://www.tampabay.com/sports/college/police-investigate-sexual-complaint-against-fsus-winston/2152335. "Florida State QB Jameis Winston Investigated for Sexual Assault, TMZ.com, November 13, 2013, http://www.tmz.com/2013/11/13/jameis-winston-florida-state-quarterback-investigated-sexual-assault/.

3 "Sexual Violence on Campus: How Too Many Institutions of High Education Are Failing to Protect Students," July 9, 2014, US Senate Subcommittee on Financial and Contracting Oversight.

4 Jeff Benedict and Armen Keteyian, *The System: The Glory and Scandal of Big-Time College Football* (New York: Doubleday, 2013), p. 74.

5 "Prevalence and Characteristics of Sexual Violence, Stalking, and Intimate Partner Violence Victimization—National Intimate Partner and Sexual Violence Survey, United States, 2011," http://www.cdc.gov/mmwr/preview/mmwrhtml/ss6308a1.htm.

6 http://rainn.org/get-information/statistics/sexual-assault-victims.

7 Callie Marie Rennison, "Privilege, Among Rape Victims," *New York Times,* December 21, 2014, http://www.nytimes.com/2014/12/22/opinion/who-suffers-most-from-rape-and-sexual-assault-in-america.html/.

8 Rakesh Kochhar and Richard Fry, "Wealth Inequality Has Widened Along Racial, Ethnic Lines Since End of Great Recession," Pew Research Center, December 12, 2014, http://www.pewresearch.org/fact-tank/2014/12/12/racial-wealth-gaps-great-recession/.

9 http://nces.ed.gov/fastfacts/display.asp?id=372.

10 Rebecca Klein, "Poverty the Strongest Factor in Which Graduates Go to College," *Huffington Post*, October 14, 2014, http://www.huffing-

tonpost.com/2014/10/14/poverty-college-enrollment_n_5978646. html.

11 http://www.chitaskforce.org/policy-recommendations/reporting-on-rape-and-sexual-violence/.

12 https://www.fbi.gov/about-us/cjis/ucr/crime-in-the-u.s/2013/crime-in-the-u.s.-2013/violent-crime/rape.

Chapter 1

13 Wade Davis, "Russell Tovey, Sexism, and Imaginary Masculinity," *Advocate*, March 4, 2015, http://www.advocate.com/commentary/2015/03/04/op-ed-russell-tovey-sexism-and-imaginary-masculinity.

14 Mike Messner, Darnell Hunt, Michele Dunbar, Perry Chen, Joan Lapp, and Patti Miller, "Boys to Men—Sports Media Messages About Masculinity," *Children Now*, September 1999, p. 11.

15 Andre Perry, "The NFL Killed Masculinity. Can Players Ever Reclaim It?" *Good*, March 1, 2014, https://www.good.is/articles/the-nfl-killed-masculinity-can-players-ever-reclaim-it.

16 Peggy Reeves Sanday, *Fraternity Gang Rape: Sex, Brotherhood, and Privilege on Campus* (New York: New York University Press, 2007), p. 7.

17 Joann Stevens, "Six Football Players and a Coach Who Cared," *New York Times*, December 5, 1976.

18 Melinda Henneberger, "Reported Sexual Assault at Notre Dame Campus Leaves More Questions than Answers," *National Catholic Reporter*, March 26, 2012, http://ncronline.org/news/accountability/reported-sexual-assault-notre-dame-campus-leaves-more-questions-answers.

19 "Four Indicted on Sex Charge," *New York Times*, September 6, 1980.

20 Katy Williams, "Ky. Considers Replacing Curci with Allen: Kentucky, Allen Discuss Job," *Washington Post*, July 11, 1981.

21 "UC Berkeley Rape Suspects Must Apologize to Victim," Associated Press, November 22, 1986, http://www.apnewsarchive.com/1986/UC-Berkeley-Rape-Suspects-Must-Apologize-to-Victim/id-022a3e798801ff9bb6c38a6e79026126.

22 Danny Robbins, "Invincible No More: Nigel Clay Planned to Be in the NFL, But Now He Is Playing for a Correctional Center," *Los Angeles Times*, February 2, 1992, http://articles.latimes.com/1992-02-02/sports/sp-2041_1_nigel-clay.

23 Dan Le Batard and Ken Rodriguez, "Hurricanes: Eye of the Storm—A Program in Disarray," *Miami Herald*, May 19, 1995. "Tennessee Drops Assault Inquiry," Associated Press, October 20, 1990, http://www.nytimes.com/1990/10/20/sports/college-football-tennessee-drops-as-

sault-inquiry.html. "Two Acquitted of Rape Charge," Associated Press, January 27, 1993, http://www.nytimes.com/1993/01/27/sports/sports-people-college-football-2-acquitted-of-rape-charge.html. "Cases Involving Athletes and Sexual Assault," *USA Today*, December 21, 2003, http://usatoday30.usatoday.com/sports/2003-12-22-athletes-assault-side_x.htm. Nina Bernstein, "Civil Rights Lawsuit in Rape Case Challenges Integrity of a Campus," *New York Times*, February 11, 1996, http://www.nytimes.com/1996/02/11/us/civil-rights-lawsuit-in-rape-case-challenges-integrity-of-a-campus.html?pagewanted=all&src=pm.

24 "Idaho State Students Accuse School of Bias—Two Plead Guilty, Are Booted from Team," Associated Press, October 11, 1995.

25 "Grambling Expels Players Charged with Rape," Associated Press, December 6, 1996, http://www.apnewsarchive.com/1996/Grambling-Expels-Players-Charged-With-Rape/id-ce6c307caa48c00476a-4b785ebc43120. David Forbes, "Shut Up and Pay," *nsfwcorp*, April 9, 2013, https://www.nsfwcorp.com/dispatch/shut-up-and-pay/. "Timeline: Colorado Recruiting Scandal," Associated Press, May 27, 2004, http://espn.go.com/ncf/news/story?id=1803891. John Canzano, "Sixteen Years After Oregon State Football Gang-Rape Allegation, Brenda Tracy Steps from the Shadows," *Oregonian*, November 14, 2014, http://www.oregonlive.com/sports/oregonian/john_canzano/index.ssf/2014/11/canzano_her_name_is_brenda_tra.html.

26 Harvey Araton, "A Woman Takes on the System," *New York Times*, July 31, 2001, http://www.nytimes.com/2001/07/31/sports/ncaafootball/31ARAT.html.

27 Bruce Feldman, "Out of Control," *ESPN the Magazine*, May 20, 2002, http://espn.go.com/magazine/vol5no12uab.html.

28 "At Naval Academy, Rape Case Casts Cloud on Military Justice," *Washington Post*, April 11, 2001, http://articles.latimes.com/2001/apr/11/news/mn-49602. Christopher Flores, "When Athletes Are Accused," *Chronicle of Higher Education*, April 19, 2002. Jason Kelly, "ND Faulted in Sexual Assault Case in 2002," *South Bend Tribune*, November 2, 2006. Stephen Gurr, "UGA Football Player Facing Rape Charges," *Athens Banner-Herald*, August 22, 2002, http://onlineathens.com/stories/082202/new_20020822070.shtml.

29 Jesse Hyde and Tad Walch, "Four Former Y. Players Indicted in Scandal," *Deseret News*, December 4, 2004, http://www.deseretnews.com/article/595110063/4-former-Y-players-indicted-in-scandal.html. "Six Tenn. Football Players Charged with Gang Rape," Associated Press, November 9, 2005, http://www.foxnews.com/story/2005/11/09/six-tenn-football-players-charged-with-gang-rape.html. Brad Wolverton,

"Three SUNY-Albany Football Players Charged with Rape," *Chronicle of Higher Education*, November 3, 2006, http://chronicle.com/article/3-SUNY-Albany-Football-Players/18083. "Cedric Everson Faces Up to 25 Years," *ESPN the Magazine*, January 11, 2011, http://espn.go.com/ncf/news/story?id=6012358. "Minnesota Football Players Released from Custody Amid Rape Probe," Associated Press, April 9, 2007, http://usatoday30.usatoday.com/sports/college/football/bigten/2007-04-09-minnesota-investigation_N.htm.

[30] Tom Farrey and Nicole Noren, "Mizzou Did Not Pursue Alleged Assault," *ESPN the Magazine*, January 24, 2014, http://espn.go.com/espn/otl/story/_/id/10323102/university-missouri-officials-did-not-pursue-rape-case-lines-investigation-finds. Jack Healy, "Accusation in Montana of Treating Rape Lightly Stirs Unlikely Public Fight," *New York Times*, April 12, 2014, http://www.nytimes.com/2014/04/13/us/accusation-in-montana-of-treating-rape-lightly-stirs-unlikely-public-fight.html?_r=0. Lucinda Shen, "Appalachian State Reconsiders Sexual Assault Policy," *Daily Tarheel*, September 26, 2012, http://www.dailytarheel.com/article/2012/09/appalachian-reconsiders-sexual-assault-policy.

[31] Billy Shields, "McGill Campus Football Team at Centre of Sex Assault Controversy," *Global News*, November 22, 2013, http://globalnews.ca/news/985364/mcgill-campus-football-team-the-centre-of-sex-assault-controversy. "Two Football Players Accused of Raping Three Women," WLTX, March 31, 2012, http://www.wltx.com/story/news/2014/02/07/1628548/. Anita Blanton, "Former ODU Football Players Sentenced for Sexual Assault," WAVY, August 25, 2014, http://wavy.com/2014/08/25/former-odu-football-players-sentenced-for-sexual-assault/. Annys Shin, "Three Former Naval Academy Football Players Face Accuser at Hearing on Rape Charges," *Washington Post*, August 27, 2013, https://www.washingtonpost.com/local/three-former-naval-academy-football-players-face-accuser-at-hearing-on-rape-charges/2013/08/27/ffb6607c-0f23-11e3-85b6-d27422650fd5_story.html. Christian Corona, "Case McCoy and Jordan Hicks to Be Reinstated, Attorney Says No Charges Will Be Filed," *Daily Texan*, January 13, 2014, http://www.dailytexanonline.com/sports/2013/01/13/case-mccoy-and-jordan-hicks-to-be-reinstated-attorney-says-no-charges-will-be. "Multiple Ohio State Football Players Investigated for Alleged Rape," WBNS-10TV, March 13, 2013, http://www.10tv.com/content/stories/2013/03/13/columbus-multiple-ohio-state-university-football-players-investigated-for-alleged-rape.html. Jessica Luther, "A Look at Complex Vanderbilt Rape Case that Left a Community Reeling," *Sports Illustrated*, February 10, 2015, http://www.si.com/

college-football/2015/02/09/vanderbilt-rape-case-brandon-vanden-burg-cory-batey. "Brown Players Under Investigation," Associated Press, June 13, 2014, http://espn.go.com/college-football/story/_/id/11079127/brown-football-players-accused-sexual-assault.

32 Ron Carrion, "New Mexico Lobos Football: Crusoe Gongbay and SaQwan Edwards Reinstated," *SB Nation*, Dan Zinski, August 12, 2014, http://www.mwcconnection.com/2014/8/12/5997501/new-mexico-lobos-football-crusoe-gongbay-and-saqwan-edwards-re-instated. Brian Hamacher, "Two University of Miami Football Play-ers Arrested for Sexual Battery," NBC 6 South Florida, July 8, 2014, http://www.nbcmiami.com/news/local/2-University-of-Miami-Foot-ball-Players-Arrested-for-Sexual-Battery-266234081.html. "Texas Longhorns Dismiss Kendall Sanders, Montrel Meander," *Fansided*, Au-gust 3, 2014, http://fansided.com/2014/08/03/texas-longhorns-dis-miss-kendall-sanders-montrel-meander/. Jerry Hinnen, "A.J. Johnson, Michael Williams Plead Not Guilty in Tennessee Rape Case," CBS Sports, March 9, 2015.

33 Walt Bogdanich, "Reporting Rape, and Wishing She Hadn't," *New York Times*, July 12, 2014, http://www.nytimes.com/2014/07/13/us/how-one-college-handled-a-sexual-assault-complaint.html. Jessica Lu-ther, "A Look at Complex Vanderbilt Rape Case that Left a Communi-ty Reeling," *Sports Illustrated*, February 10, 2015, http://www.si.com/college-football/2015/02/09/vanderbilt-rape-case-brandon-vanden-burg-cory-batey.

34 "Florida Goes to Court," *New York Times*, September 5, 1984, http://www.nytimes.com/1984/09/05/sports/sports-people-florida-goes-to-court.html. Stan Grossfield, "A Voice for the Victims," *Boston Globe*, June 16, 2004, http://www.boston.com/sports/other_sports/arti-cles/2004/06/16/a_voice_for_the_victims/. Tom Ley, "Former Mich-igan Kicker Expelled for Sexual Misconduct," *Deadspin*, January 29, 2014, http://deadspin.com/former-michigan-kicker-expelled-for-sex-ual-misconduct-1511488287. Melinda Henneberger, "Reported Sex-ual Assault at Notre Dame Campus Leaves More Questions than An-swers," *National Catholic Reporter*, March 26, 2012, http://ncronline.org/news/accountability/reported-sexual-assault-notre-dame-cam-pus-leaves-more-questions-answers.

35 Sarah E. Ullman, "Multiple Perpetrator Rape Victimization: How It Differs and Why It Matters," in *Handbook on the Study of Multiple Perpetrator Rape*, eds. Miranda A.H. Horvath and Jessica Woodhams (New York: Routledge, 2013), p. 198.

36 Joann Stevens, "Six Football Players and a Coach Who Cared," *New York Times*, December 5, 1976. Steve Henson, "Bradley Shows that

Seeing Is Believing," *Los Angeles Times*, August 31, 1996, http://articles.latimes.com/1996-08-31/sports/sp-39488_1_freddie-bradley. Alan Tieuli, "Couldn't Rego Mess Have Been Avoided?" IrishEyes.com, October 11, 2001, http://www.scout.com/college/notre-dame/story/20323-why-has-rego-mess-lingered. Rich Cimini, "Abram Elam Aiming for Fresh Start," *Daily News*, November 25, 2007, http://www.nydailynews.com/sports/football/jets/abram-elam-aiming-fresh-start-article-1.256970. "Cedric Everson Faces Up to 25 years," ESPN, January 11, 2011, http://espn.go.com/ncf/news/story?id=6012358. Chris Monter, "E. J. Jones Gets New Start at Illinois State," *Gopher Digest*, October 5, 2008, http://www.scout.com/college/minnesota/story/797723-e-j-jones-gets-new-start-at-illinois-state. "Keith Massey—2010 Football," Kentucky State Football, http://www.ksuthorobreds.com/roster.aspx?path=&rp_id=9. Antonya English, "Cincinnati Bearcats' Alex Daniels Has Renewed his Life," *Tampa Bay Times*, December 29, 2009, http://www.tampabay.com/sports/college/cincinnati-bearcats-alex-daniels-has-renewed-his-life/1061967. Cortez Strickland, "Running Back Derrick Washington Talks About Time in Prison," *USA Today*, January 17, 2013, http://www.usatoday.com/story/sports/ncaaf/2013/01/17/derrick-washington-tuskegee-missouri/1842843/. Jessica Luther, "A Look at Complex Vanderbilt Rape Case that Left a Community Reeling," *Sports Illustrated*, February 10, 2015, http://www.si.com/college-football/2015/02/09/vanderbilt-rape-case-brandon-vandenburg-cory-batey.

[37] Jessica Luther, "The Wrestler and the Rape Victim," *Vice Sports*, December 15, 2014, https://sports.vice.com/en_us/article/the-wrestler-and-the-rape-victim.

[38] Joel Anderson, "Can Green-Beckham Be Trusted?" *ESPN the Magazine*, April 29, 2015, http://espn.go.com/nfl/story/_/id/12782255/can-dorial-green-beckham-trusted. Jon Rothstein, "Humbled by Past Mistakes, Brandon Austin Seeks Another Chance," CBS Sports, May 29, 2015, http://www.cbssports.com/collegebasketball/eye-on-college-basketball/25199618/humbled-by-past-mistakes-brandon-austin-seeks-another-chance.

[39] Bryan Denson, "Woman Sues OSU, Ex-Head Football Coach Mike Riley, Says Her 1999 Rape Occurred in 'Sexually Violent Culture,'" *Oregonian*, September 1, 2015, http://www.oregonlive.com/pacific-northwest-news/index.ssf/2015/09/woman_sues_osu_football_coach.html. Christian Corona, "Case McCoy and Jordan Hicks to Be Reinstated, Attorney Says No Charges Will Be Filed," *Daily Texan*, January 13, 2014, http://www.dailytexanonline.com/sports/2013/01/13/case-mccoy-and-jordan-hicks-to-be-reinstated-attorney-says-no-charges-will-

be. "Texas Longhorns Dismiss Kendall Sanders, Montrel Meander," *Fansided*, August 3, 2014, http://fansided.com/2014/08/03/texas-longhorns-dismiss-kendall-sanders-montrel-meander/. Jessica Luther, "A Look at Complex Vanderbilt Rape Case that Left a Community Reeling," *Sports Illustrated*, February 10, 2015, http://www.si.com/college-football/2015/02/09/vanderbilt-rape-case-brandon-vandenburg-cory-batey.

40 Jed S. Rakoff, "Why Innocent People Plead Guilty," *New York Review of Books*, November 20, 2014, http://www.nybooks.com/articles/2014/11/20/why-innocent-people-plead-guilty/.

41 Marissa Payne, "Erica Kinsman, Who Accused Jameis Winston of Rape, Tells Her Story in New Documentary *The Hunting Ground*," *Washington Post*, February 19, 2015, https://www.washingtonpost.com/news/early-lead/wp/2015/02/19/erica-kinsman-who-accused-jameis-winston-of-rape-tells-her-story-in-new-documentary-the-hunting-ground/.

42 Stassa Edwards, "Steubenville Redux: Victim Blaming in a Florida Football Town," *Ms. Magazine*, November 22, 2013, http://msmagazine.com/blog/2013/11/22/steubenville-redux-victim-blaming-in-a-florida-football-town/.

43 Adam Weinstein, "Jameis Winston Isn't the Only Problem Here: An FSU Teacher's Lament," *Deadspin*, November 21, 2013, http://deadspin.com/jameis-winston-isnt-the-only-problem-here-an-fsu-teac-1467707410.

44 Marci Robin, "The Sorority House I Lived in at FSU Is Getting Bomb Threats Over the Jameis Winston Rape Case, And I'm Not Surprised," *xoJane*, November 25, 2015, http://www.xojane.com/issues/delta-zeta-fsu-tallahassee-jameis-winston-rape-accusation.

45 Alan Schmadtke, "FSU Kicker Fined After Taping Sexual Encounter," *Orlando Sentinel*, May 17, 1994, http://articles.orlandosentinel.com/1994-05-17/sports/9405170059_1_bentley-bates-florida-state.

46 Alan Schmadtke, "Florida State Reserve Arrested," *Orlando Sentinel*, May 18, 1994.

47 Patrick Sauer, "I Was Shot and Raped By an FSU Player. I Still Cheer for the Seminoles," *Deadspin*, April 17, 2014, http://deadspin.com/i-was-shot-and-raped-by-an-fsu-player-i-still-cheer-fo-1563858521.

48 Rich Mckay and Josh Robbins, "FSU Tried to Protect Player in Rape Case," *Orlando Sentinel*, August 15, 2003, http://articles.orlandosentinel.com/2003-08-15/news/0308150381_1_wetherell-travis-johnson-president-of-student.

49 Walt Bogdanich, "FSU Reported Few Rape Cases to the US," *New York Times*, November 25, 2015, http://www.nytimes.com/2015/11/26/sports/ncaafootball/fsu-reported-few-rape-cases-to-the-us.html.

Chapter 2

50 Gene Williams, "Travis Johnson Arrested," Warchant.com, April 10, 2003, https://florida.rivals.com/content.asp?CID=179878.

51 Brian Landman, "Testimony in FSU Case Draws Tears," *St. Petersburg Times*, August 14, 2003, http://www.sptimes.com/2003/08/14/news_pf/Sports/Testimony_in_FSU_case.shtml.

52 Rich Mckay and Josh Robbins, "FSU Tried to Protect Player in Rape Case," *Orlando Sentinel*, August 15, 2003, http://articles.orlandosentinel.com/2003-08-15/news/0308150381_1_wetherell-travis-johnson-president-of-student.

53 Josh Robbins, "Johnson Is Found Not Guilty of Sexual Assault," *Sun-Sentinel*, August 15, 2003, http://articles.sun-sentinel.com/2003-08-15/sports/0308150164_1_johnson-s-right-arm-mr-johnson-johnson-s-attorneys.

54 Josh Robbins, "FSU Player Quickly Wins Acquittal on Sex Charge," *Orlando Sentinel*, August 15, 2003, http://articles.orlandosentinel.com/2003-08-15/news/0308150382_1_johnson-tallahassee-florida-state.

55 https://www.floridamemory.com/photographiccollection/photo_exhibits/civil-rights/.

56 Karl Etters, "'KKK' Painted on Third Wakulla Church," *Tallahassee Democrat*, December 10, 2014, http://www.tallahassee.com/story/news/breaking/2014/12/10/third-wakulla-church-vandalized-with-racist-remarks/20220935.

57 Karl Etters, "KKK Wizard Confirms Fliers Were Targeted Effort," *Tallahassee Democrat*, March 18, 2015, http://www.tallahassee.com/story/news/2015/03/17/kkk-fliers-false-concern-experts-say/24907821/.

58 Alex Gaskin, "Letter to the Editor: FSU Can Be More Inclusive to Minority Students," FSUNews.com, December 2, 2015, http://www.fsunews.com/story/opinion/2015/12/02/tomahawk-chop-racism/76663624/.

59 Joe Schad, "When to Hold 'Em, When to Fold 'Em," *Sun-Sentinel*, July 6, 2003, http://articles.sun-sentinel.com/2003-07-06/sports/0307060141_1_adrian-mcpherson-teddy-dupay-gambling-charges.

60 Christopher Hartley and Linh Vuong, "Created Equal: Racial and Ethnic Disparities in the US Criminal Justice System," *National Council on Crime and Delinquency*, March 2009, p. 2.

61 Jessica Luther, "The NFL's Domestic Violence Problem and Our Race Problem," *Vice Sports*, September 25, 2014, https://sports.vice.com/en_

us/article/the-nfls-domestic-violence-problem-and-our-race-problem.

62 Lisa Lindquist Dorr, *White Women, Rape, and the Power of Race in Virginia, 1900–1960* (Chapel Hill: The University of North Carolina Press, 2004), location 192 (Kindle).

63 Jamelle Bouie, "The Deadly History of 'They're Raping Our Women,'" *Slate*, June 18, 2015, http://www.slate.com/articles/news_and_politics/history/2015/06/the_deadly_history_of_they_re_raping_our_women_racists_have_long_defended.html.

64 Samuel Gross and Michael Shaffer, "Exonerations in the United States, 1989–2012," *National Registry of Exonerations*, June 2012.

65 Byron Hurt, "Rape, A Loaded Issue for Black Men," *NewBlackMan (in Exile)*, December 5, 2013, http://www.newblackmaninexile.net/2013/12/rape-loaded-issue-for-black-men-on.html.

66 Elizabeth Stoker Bruenig, "Why Americans Don't Care About Prison Rape," *Nation*, March 2, 2015, http://www.thenation.com/article/why-americans-dont-care-about-prison-rape/.

67 Kirsten West Savali, "Rape Culture: Why Prison Rape Needs to Be a Part of the Discussion," *Root*, January 12, 2016, http://www.theroot.com/articles/culture/2016/01/rape_culture_why_prison_rape_needs_to_be_a_part_of_the_discussion.html.

68 Patrick Sauer, "I Was Shot and Raped by an FSU Player. I Still Cheer for the Seminoles," *Deadspin*, April 17, 2014, http://deadspin.com/i-was-shot-and-raped-by-an-fsu-player-i-still-cheer-fo-1563858521.

69 Cork Gaines, "College Football Reaches Record $3.4 Billion in Revenue," *Business Insider*, December 17, 2014, http://www.businessinsider.com/college-football-revenue-2014-12.

70 Steve Berkowitz, "Tax Return Shows SEC Made $527.4 Million in First Year of CFP, SEC Network," *USA Today*, January 19, 2016, http://www.usatoday.com/story/sports/college/2016/01/19/sec-tax-return-college-football-playoff-sec-network-mike-slive/79006606/.

71 Chris Smith, "College Football's Most Valuable Teams 2015: Texas, Notre Dame, and . . . Tennessee?" *Forbes*, December 22, 2015, http://www.forbes.com/sites/chrissmith/2015/12/22/college-footballs-most-valuable-teams-2015-texas-notre-dame-and-tennessee/#2715e-4857a0b445345065130.

72 "NCAA Salaries: NCAAF Coaches," *USA Today*, http://sports.usatoday.com/ncaa/salaries/.

73 "NCAA Salaries: NCAA Athletic Directors," *USA Today*, http://sports.usatoday.com/ncaa/salaries/all/director.

74 Peter Jacobs, "The 10 Highest-Paid College Presidents," *Forbes*, December 7, 2014, http://www.businessinsider.com/highest-paid-college-presidents-2014-12.

[75] Steve Berkowitz, "Emmert Made $1.7 Million, According to NCAA Tax Return," *USA Today*, July 14, 2013, http://www.usatoday.com/story/sports/college/2013/07/10/ncaa-mark-emmert-salary-million-tax-return/2505667/.

[76] Will Hobson and Steven Rich, "In the Red," *Washington Post*, November 23, 2015, http://www.washingtonpost.com/sf/sports/wp/2015/11/23/running-up-the-bills/.

[77] Sally Jenkins, "Those Who Run College Sports Don't Look Much Like Those Who Play College Sports," *USA Today*, April 9, 2015, https://www.washingtonpost.com/sports/colleges/those-who-run-college-sports-dont-look-like-those-who-play-college-sports/2015/04/09/70d3ae00-dec5-11e4-a500-1c5bb1d8ff6a_story.html.

[78] Shaun R. Harper, Collin D. Williams Jr., and Horatio W. Blackman, "Black Male Student-Athletes and Racial Inequalities in NCAA Division I College Sports," University of Pennsylvania, Center for the Study of Race and Equity in Education, p. 3.

[79] Kareem Abdul-Jabbar, "College Athletes of the World, Unite," *Jacobin*, November 12, 2014, https://www.jacobinmag.com/2014/11/college-athletes-of-the-world-unite/.

[80] Shaun R. Harper, Collin D. Williams Jr., and Horatio W. Blackman, "Black Male Student-Athletes and Racial Inequalities in NCAA Division I College Sports," University of Pennsylvania, Center for the Study of Race and Equity in Education.

[81] Taylor Branch, "The Shame of College Sports," *Atlantic*, October 2011, http://www.theatlantic.com/magazine/archive/2011/10/the-shame-of-college-sports/308643/.

Chapter 3

[82] http://knowyourix.org/title-ix/title-ix-the-basics/.

[83] "Sexual Violence on Campus: How Too Many Institutions of High Education Are Failing to Protect Students," July 9, 2014, US Senate Subcommittee on Financial and Contracting Oversight.

[84] "Injured Top College Athletes Should Not Carry the Costs, Says Majority . . . Americans Divide Over College Degrees in Sports," Marist Poll, March 24, 2015, http://maristpoll.marist.edu/tag/hbo-real-sports/.

[85] Stan Grossfield, "A Voice for the Victims," *Boston Globe*, June 16, 2004, http://www.boston.com/sports/other_sports/articles/2004/06/16/a_voice_for_the_victims/.

[86] Ken Armstrong, "Jury Upholds UW in Handling of Rape Allegation Against Ex-Player," *Seattle Times*, November 5, 2009, http://www.

seattletimes.com/sports/uw-huskies/jury-upholds-uw-in-handling-of-rape-allegation-against-ex-player/.

87 Tom Ley, "Former Michigan Kicker Expelled for Sexual Misconduct," *Deadspin*, January 29, 2014, http://deadspin.com/former-michigan-kicker-expelled-for-sexual-misconduct-1511488287.

88 Walt Bogdanich, "Reporting Rape, and Wishing She Hadn't," *New York Times*, July 12, 2014, http://www.nytimes.com/2014/07/13/us/how-one-college-handled-a-sexual-assault-complaint.html.

89 Patrick Brown, "Butch Jones: Pearson Situation 'Not an Indication of What We Have,'" *Times Free Press*, April 25, 2015, http://www.timesfreepress.com/news/sports/college/story/2015/apr/25/butch-jones-pearson-situation-not-indication-what-we-have/300829/.

90 John Keilman, "Police Escorts for Sports Teams a 'Troubling' Privilege, Critics Say," *Chicago Tribune*, December 21, 2014, http://www.chicagotribune.com/suburbs/lake-forest/ct-police-escorts-sports-met-20141220-story.html.

91 Pat Forde, "Troopers Protect the Coach—and a Little More," ESPN, October 21, 2006, http://espn.go.com/espn/columns/story?id=2631660.

92 Paula Lavigne, "Lawyers, Status, Public Backlash Aid College Athletes Accused of Crimes," ESPN, June 15, 2015, http://espn.go.com/espn/otl/story/_/id/13065247/college-athletes-major-programs-benefit-confluence-factors-somes-avoid-criminal-charges.

93 Josh Peter, "Former Oklahoma Coach Barry Switzer Admits He Covered Up Minor Charges Against Players," *USA Today*, October 9, 2014, http://ftw.usatoday.com/2014/10/barry-switzer-misdemeanor-charges.

94 Bruce Feldman, "Out of Control," *ESPN the Magazine*, May 20, 2002, http://espn.go.com/magazine/vol5no12uab.html.

95 Melinda Henneberger, "Reported Sexual Assault at Notre Dame Campus Leaves More Questions than Answers," *National Catholic Reporter*, March 26, 2012, http://ncronline.org/news/accountability/reported-sexual-assault-notre-dame-campus-leaves-more-questions-answers.

96 American Humane Association, "Facts About Animal Abuse and Domestic Violence," http://www.americanhumane.org/interaction/support-the-bond/fact-sheets/animal-abuse-domestic-violence.html.

97 Mike McIntire and Walt Bogdanich, "At Florida State, Football Clouds Justice," *New York Times*, October 10, 2014, http://www.nytimes.com/2014/10/12/us/florida-state-football-casts-shadow-over-tallahassee-justice.html.

98 Martin Kinston, "'*60 Minutes Sports*' Looks at Allegations of Rape, Cover-Up At UM," *Missourian*, November 5, 2014, http://missoulian.com/helena/news/local/minutes-sports-looks-at-allegations-of-rape-

cover-up-at/article_edfefc50-1fd4-57bc-a746-55561a2f760d.html.

[99] Jon Krakauer, *Missoula: Rape and the Justice System in a College Town* (New York: Doubleday, 2015).

[100] "Jordan Johnson Acquitted of Rape," Associated Press, March 4, 2013, http://espn.go.com/college-football/story/_/id/9006061/former-montana-grizzlies-quarterback-jordan-johnson-acquitted-rape.

[101] "Robin Pflugrad Defends Montana," Associated Press, July 27, 2013, http://espn.go.com/college-football/story/_/id/9514039/ex-montana-grizzlies-coach-robin-pflugrad-defends-program.

[102] Lester Munson, "Landmark Settlement in ASU Rape Case," ESPN, January 30, 2009, http://espn.go.com/espn/print?id=3871666.

[103] David Wharton, "A Shot in the Dark," *Los Angeles Times*, August 25, 2005, http://articles.latimes.com/2005/aug/25/sports/sp-wade25.

[104] John Dougherty, "Into the Fire," *Phoenix New Times*, September 6, 2007, http://www.phoenixnewtimes.com/news/into-the-fire-6404613.

[105] "Hakim Hill Returns to Scene of Troubled Past," ESPN, September 15, 2003, http://sports.espn.go.com/espn/wire?id=1616707.

[106] "Hakim Hill, Booted from Arizona State, Will Play at Northern Iowa," *Courier*, January 21, 2005, http://wcfcourier.com/panthermania.net/news/news/football/hakim-hill-booted-from-arizona-state-will-play-at-northern/article_4f71dde3-9b26-5a5b-8627-ff34fe361714.html.

[107] Part of this section appeared in an earlier form in Jessica Luther, "Missouri Football's Rape Culture 'and So on and So Forth,'" *Vice Sports*, September 9, 2014, https://sports.vice.com/en_us/article/missouri-footballs-rape-culture-and-so-on-and-so-forth.

[108] Tom Farrey and Nicole Noren, "Mizzou Did Not Pursue Alleged Assault," ESPN, January 24, 2014, http://espn.go.com/espn/otl/story/_/id/10323102/university-missouri-officials-did-not-pursue-rape-case-lines-investigation-finds. Paula Lavigne and Nicole Noren, "Athletes, Assaults and Inaction," ESPN, August 25, 2014, http://espn.go.com/espn/otl/story/_/id/11381416/missouri-tulsa-southern-idaho-face-allegations-did-not-investigate-title-ix-cases.

[109] Jeff Benedict and Armen Keteyian, *The System: The Glory and Scandal of Big-Time College Football* (New York City: Doubleday, 2013), p. 175.

[110] Sarah D. Wire, "Former Football Player Pleads Guilty to Sexual Misconduct," *Maneater*, October 11, 2005, http://www.themaneater.com/stories/2005/10/11/former-football-player-pleads-guilty-sexual-miscon/.

[111] Wade Livingston, "Post-Practice Discussion Part of Sexual Assault Reporting Conversation at MU," *Missourian*, August 26, 2014,

http://www.columbiamissourian.com/sports/post-practice-discussion-part-of-sexual-assault-reporting-conversation-at/article_0bc-f312a-93cb-5308-a5be-a2e6117753f4.html.

112 "FSU Announces Settlement in Erica Kinsman Matter," *FSU*, January 25, 2016, http://news.fsu.edu/More-FSU-News/FSU-announces-settlement-in-Erica-Kinsman-matter.

113 Joe Nocera, "After Settlement, Florida State Shows Sympathy for Victim: Itself," *New York Times*, January 29, 2016, http://www.nytimes.com/2016/01/30/sports/ncaafootball/florida-state-protects-the-brand-but-what-about-the-students.html.

114 Kavitha A. Davidson, "Buy a Player Lunch? No. Pay to Settle His Rape Case? Sure," *Bloomberg View*, January 28, 2016, http://www.bloombergview.com/articles/2016-01-28/buy-a-player-lunch-no-pay-to-settle-his-rape-case-sure-.

Chapter 4

115 National Collegiate Athletic Association, "Membership," http://www.ncaa.org/about/who-we-are/membership.

116 Alexander Wolff, "The Fall Roundup: Persuasive Hostesses Help College Lasso Top Prospects," *Sports Illustrated*, August 31, 1987, http://www.si.com/vault/1987/08/31/116051/the-fall-roundup-persuasive-hostesses-help-colleges-lasso-top-prospects.

117 Patrick Sauer, "I Was Shot and Raped by an FSU Player. I Still Cheer for the Seminoles," *Deadspin*, April 17, 2014, http://deadspin.com/i-was-shot-and-raped-by-an-fsu-player-i-still-cheer-fo-1563858521.

118 Joe Schad, "Pretty Faces Make Good Recruiters," *Sun-Sentinel*, February 3, 2002, http://articles.sun-sentinel.com/2002-02-03/sports/0202020473_1_georgia-girls-black-dress-school-football-players.

119 Rob Moseley, "Oregon Defends Recruiting Practices," *Register-Guard*, December 20, 2002, http://www.thefreelibrary.com/Oregon+defends+recruiting+practices.-a095771228.

120 John Canzano, "Sixteen Years After Oregon State Football Gang-Rape Allegation, Brenda Tracy Steps from the Shadows," *Oregonian*, November 14, 2014, http://www.oregonlive.com/sports/oregonian/john_canzano/index.ssf/2014/11/canzano_her_name_is_brenda_tra.html.

121 Joe Watson, "Risky Behavior Not Policed in ASU Football Recruiting," *State Press*, February 25, 2003, https://asuwebdevilarchive.asu.edu/issues/2003/03/13/specialreports/339775.

122 Robbie Andreu, "Role of Gator Guides Under Scrutiny," *Gainesville Sun*, February 25, 2004, http://www.gainesville.com/article/20040225/GATORS01/40224030.

[123] Joe Watson, "Risky Behavior Not Policed in ASU Football Recruiting," *State Press*, February 25, 2003, https://asuwebdevilarchive.asu.edu/issues/2003/03/13/specialreports/339775.

[124] "Timeline: Colorado Recruiting Scandal," Associated Press, May 27, 2004, http://espn.go.com/ncf/news/story?id=1803891.

[125] Mike Freeman, "Getting a Grip on Recruiting Parties," *New York Times*, November 21, 2002, http://www.nytimes.com/2002/11/21/sports/getting-a-grip-on-recruiting-parties.html.

[126] "Barnett Forced Out; Receives $3 Million Settlement," ESPN, December 9, 2005, http://espn.go.com/college-football/news/story?id=2252252.

[127] Rick Reilly, "Another Victim at Colorado," *Sports Illustrated*, February 23, 2004, http://www.si.com/more-sports/2010/01/01/hnida.

[128] "University Asks Police to Look into Alleged Rape," CNN, February 18, 2004, http://www.cnn.com/2004/US/Central/02/18/colorado.football/.

[129] Jeff Hauser, "Gary Barnett Enthusiastic to Put the Past Behind Him at Colorado," *SB Nation*, September 15, 2015, http://www.ralphiereport.com/2015/9/15/9299767/gary-barnett-enthusiastic-to-put-the-past-behind-him-at-cu.

[130] "Report Questions Top Officials' Leadership," Associated Press, May 19, 2004, http://espn.go.com/ncf/news/story?id=1803763.

[131] "Timeline: Colorado Recruiting Scandal," Associated Press, May 27, 2004, http://espn.go.com/ncf/news/story?id=1803891.

[132] Robbie Andreu, "Role of Gator Guides Under Scrutiny," *Gainesville Sun*, February 25, 2004, http://www.gainesville.com/article/20040225/GATORS01/40224030.

[133] Jeff Pearlman, "The Tragic Story of Willie Williams, College Football's First Celebrity Recruit," *Bleacher Report*, February 4, 2014, http://bleacherreport.com/articles/1943325-the-tragic-story-of-willie-williams-college-footballs-first-celebrity-recruit.

[134] Danny Robbins, "Invincible No More: Nigel Clay Planned to Be in the NFL, But Now He Is Playing for a Correctional Center," *Los Angeles Times*, February 2, 1992, http://articles.latimes.com/1992-02-02/sports/sp-2041_1_nigel-clay.

[135] Mike Freeman, "Getting a Grip on Recruiting Parties," *New York Times*, November 21, 2002, http://www.nytimes.com/2002/11/21/sports/getting-a-grip-on-recruiting-parties.html.

[136] Pete Thamel and Thayer Evans, "NCAA Puts Tennessee's Recruiting Under Scrutiny," *New York Times*, December 8, 2009, http://www.nytimes.com/2009/12/09/sports/ncaafootball/09tennessee.html.

[137] Jeff Benedict and Armen Keteyian, *The System: The Glory and Scandal of Big-Time College Football* (New York City: Doubleday, 2013), p. 36.

138 "Special Report on Oklahoma State Football: The Overview," *Sports Illustrated*, September 10, 2013, http://www.si.com/college-football/2013/09/10/osu-introduction.

139 Parts of this section appear in an earlier form in Jessica Luther, "A Look at Complex Vanderbilt Rape Case that Left a Community Reeling," *Sports Illustrated*, February 10, 2015, http://www.si.com/college-football/2015/02/09/vanderbilt-rape-case-brandon-vandenburg-cory-batey.

140 Jack Dickey, "Vanderbilt Football Coach Will Not Hire Assistants Until He's Seen What Their Wives Look Like," *Deadspin*, May 31, 2012, http://deadspin.com/5914625/vanderbilt-football-coach-will-not-hire-assistants-until-hes-seen-what-their-wives-look-like.

141 Adam Sparks, "Vanderbilt Rape Trial Hangs Over Recruiting Weekend," *Tennessean*, January 16, 2015, http://www.tennessean.com/story/sports/college/vanderbilt/2015/01/15/vanderbilt-rape-trial-hangs-recruiting-weekend/21843459/.

142 Tom Roeder, "Report: West Point Football Team Recruited High School Athletes with Booze, Women," *Gazette*, October 25, 2014, http://gazette.com/report-west-point-football-team-recruited-high-school-athletes-with-booze-women/article/1540172.

143 Allison Sherry, "CU Settles Case Stemming from Recruit Scandal," *Denver Post*, December 6, 2007, http://www.denverpost.com/wintersports/ci_7645722.

144 Patrick Saunders and Tom Kensler, "How Colorado's Football Program Got Mired in a Decade of Losing," *Denver Post*, December 1, 2014, http://www.denverpost.com/colleges/ci_27041416/cu-buffs-football-program-tries-dig-out-deep.

145 Alex Burness, "CU Buffs' Isaiah Holland Charged with Sexual Assault, Suspended Indefinitely from Team," *Daily Camera*, January 14, 2015, http://www.dailycamera.com/cu-news/ci_27322841/cu-buffs-player-isaiah-holland-suspended-indefinitely-from.

146 Marshall Zelinger, "Fired CU Football Coach, Gary Barnett, Hired to Replace Larry Zimmer in Radio Broadcast Booth," Denver 7, August 21, 2015, http://www.thedenverchannel.com/news/local-news/fired-cu-football-coach-gary-barnett-hired-to-replace-larry-zimmer-in-radio-broadcast-booth.

147 "NCAA Releases New Handbook Addressing Sexual Assault," NCAA, September 3, 2014, http://www.ncaa.org/about/resources/media-center/news/ncaa-releases-new-handbook-addressing-sexual-assault.

Chapter 5

148 Parts of this section appeared in an earlier form in Jessica Luther,

"Who We Talk About When Athletes Are Accused of Sexual Assault," *Vice Sports*, October 14, 2014, https://sports.vice.com/en_us/article/who-we-talk-about-when-athletes-are-accused-of-sexual-assault.

149 "Treon Harris Accused of Assault," ESPN, October 10, 2014, http://espn.go.com/college-football/story/_/id/11653329/treon-harris-florida-gators-suspended-indefinitely-legal-matter.

150 https://twitter.com/AngryBlackLady/status/519224958543597568. Roger Simmons, "Text of Treon Harris Press Release Issued By His Attorney," *Orlando Sentinel*, October 9, 2014, http://www.orlandosentinel.com/sports/florida-gators/os-treon-harris-attorney-press-release-20141009-story.html.

151 Barrett Sallee, "LSU Loss Seals Jeff Driskel's Fate, Can Treon Harris Save Will Muschamp's Job?" *Bleacher Report*, October 12, 2014, http://bleacherreport.com/articles/2228498-lsu-loss-seals-jeff-driskels-fate-can-treon-harris-save-will-muschamps-job. Zach Abolverdi, "UF Quarterback Harris Ready to Get Back on Field," Gatorsports.com, October 13, 2014, http://www.gatorsports.com/article/20141013/ARTICLES/141019875/1185/frontpage?Title=UF-quarterback-Harris-looking-to-move-on.

152 Mike Bianchi, "Treon Harris Is Back As Gators QB, But Attorney Huntley Johnson Is Team MVP," *Orlando Sentinel,* October 10, 2014, http://www.orlandosentinel.com/sports/os-mike-bianchi-saturday-circus-1011-20141010-column.html.

153 Gregg Doyle, "After State Declined Chance to Judge Winston, Time for Us to Follow Suit," CBS Sports, December 5, 2013, http://www.cbssports.com/general/writer/gregg-doyel/24350241/after-state-declined-chance-to-judge-winston-time-for-us-to-follow-suit.

154 Walt Bogdanich, "A Star Player Accused, and a Flawed Rape Investigation," *New York Times*, April 16, 2014, http://www.nytimes.com/interactive/2014/04/16/sports/errors-in-inquiry-on-rape-allegations-against-fsu-jameis-winston.html.

155 Travis Haney, "Source: Manziel Questioned By NCAA," ESPN, August 27, 2013, http://espn.go.com/college-football/story/_/id/9603661/ncaa-investigators-meet-texas-johnny-manziel-6-hours-source.

156 Travis Waldron, "How to Fix the NCAA Rule That May Ensnare Johnny Manziel," *Think Progress*, August 5, 2013, http://thinkprogress.org/sports/2013/08/05/2410501/how-to-fix-the-ncaa-rule-that-may-ensnare-johnny-manziel/.

157 Kavitha A. Davidson, "Football's Head Fake on Jameis Winston's Past," *Bloomberg View*, February 26, 2015, http://www.bloombergview.com/articles/2015-02-26/football-s-head-fake-on-jameis-winston-s-past.

158 Tomas Rios, "Misplaced Priorities," *Sports on Earth*, December 7,

2013, http://www.sportsonearth.com/article/64469260/.

[159] Jonathan Drew and Allen G. Breed, "UVA Kidnap Suspect Jesse Leroy Matthew 'Doesn't Mean To Be Creepy,' Friend Says," Associated Press, December 3, 2014, http://www.huffingtonpost.com/2014/10/03/uva-kidnap-jesse-leroy-matthew_n_5929602.html.

[160] "Reporter: USC Passed on James Franklin Due to Vanderbilt Players' Ongoing Rape Case," CBS Pittsburgh, January 9, 2014, http://pittsburgh.cbslocal.com/2014/01/09/reporter-usc-passed-on-james-franklin-due-to-vanderbilt-players-ongoing-rape-case/.

[161] Gregg Doyel, "James Franklin the Right Man—and Perfect Coach—for Penn State," CBS Sports, January 9, 2014, http://www.cbssports.com/general/writer/gregg-doyel/24403448/james-franklin-the-right-man-and-perfect-coach-for-penn-state.

[162] Jeff Hauser, "Brendan Schaub: A Long Way from Boulder, Still a Buff for Life," *SB Nation*, May 18, 2015, http://www.ralphiereport.com/2015/5/18/8588911/brendan-schaub-a-long-way-from-boulder-still-a-buff-for-life.

[163] Jeff Hauser, "Gary Barnett Enthusiastic to Put the Past Behind Him at Colorado," *SB Nation*, September 15, 2015, http://www.ralphiereport.com/2015/9/15/9299767/gary-barnett-enthusiastic-to-put-the-past-behind-him-at-cu.

[164] Parts of this section appeared in an earlier form in Jessica Luther, "A Look at Complex Vanderbilt Rape Case that Left a Community Reeling," *Sports Illustrated*, February 10, 2015, http://www.si.com/college-football/2015/02/09/vanderbilt-rape-case-brandon-vandenburg-cory-batey.

[165] Stacey Barchenger, "Judge Grants Mistrial in Vanderbilt Rape Case," *Tennessean*, June 24, 2015, http://www.tennessean.com/story/news/crime/2015/06/23/judge-rules-vanderbilt-rape-mistrial/29135323/.

[166] Sean Newell, "I Held Up the 'Hi Lizzy Seeberg' Sign on ESPN's *GameDay*. Here's Why," *Deadspin*, September 8, 2013, http://deadspin.com/i-held-up-the-hi-lizzy-seeberg-sign-on-espns-gameday-1271410289.

Part 2

[167] "Oregon Players Chant 'No Means No' After Beating Florida State," *SI Wire*, January 1, 2015, http://www.si.com/si-wire/2015/01/01/oregon-florida-state-no-means-no-chant.

[168] Kate Fagan, "News & Commentary: Why Taunting a Football Player with 'No Means No' Is a Terrible Idea," ESPNW, January 2, 2015, http://espn.go.com/espnw/news-commentary/article/12111864/why-taunting-football-player-no-means-no-terrible-idea.

[169] Jessica Luther, "Jameis Winston Conduct Hearing Transcript Reveals Mass Confusion and Bizarre Decision-Making," *Vice Sports*, December 31, 2014, https://sports.vice.com/en_us/article/jameis-winston-conduct-hearing-transcript-reveals-mass-confusion-and-bizarre-decision-making.

[170] John Canzano, "Sixteen Years After Oregon State Football Gang-Rape Allegation, Brenda Tracy Steps from the Shadows," *Oregonian*, November 14, 2014, http://www.oregonlive.com/sports/oregonian/john_canzano/index.ssf/2014/11/canzano_her_name_is_brenda_tra.html.

[171] T. Christian Miller and Ryan Gabrielsson, "Upon Further Review: Inside the Police Failure to Stop Darren Sharper's Rape Spree," ProPublica, April 8, 2015, https://www.propublica.org/article/police-fail-stop-nfl-darren-sharper-rape-spree.

[172] "Prosecutors Won't Press Charges Against Roberson," Associated Press, January 8, 2004.

[173] "Suit Comes After Criminal Charges Weren't Filed," Associated Press, October 28, 2003.

[174] Jessica Luther, "Fighting Sexual Assault," *Austin Chronicle*, May 16, 2014, http://www.austinchronicle.com/news/2014-05-16/fighting-sexual-assault/.

[175] Reina A.E. Gattuso, "Do You Think I'm Pretty?" *Harvard Crimson*, February 27, 2015, http://www.thecrimson.com/column/material-girl/article/2015/2/27/you-think-im-pretty/.

[176] Rebecca Traister, "The Game Is Rigged," *New York Magazine*, October 19, 2015, http://nymag.com/thecut/2015/10/why-consensual-sex-can-still-be-bad.html.

[177] https://www.uhs.uga.edu/consent/.

[178] Matt Baker, "Jameis Winston Case: Attorneys Dispute $7 Million Settlement Talk," *Tampa Bay Times*, September 24, 2014, http://www.tampabay.com/sports/college/jameis-winstons-advisor-accuser-wanted-7-million/2199164.

[179] Mike Florio, "Lawsuit Against Winston Refers to Second Victim," *ProFootballTalk*, April 16, 2015, http://profootballtalk.nbcsports.com/2015/04/16/lawsuit-against-winston-refers-to-second-victim/.

[180] http://nij.gov/multimedia/presenter/presenter-campbell/pages/presenter-campbell-transcript.aspx

[181] Kimberly A. Lonsway, Joanne Archambault, and David Lisak, "False Reports: Moving Beyond the Issue to Successfully Investigate and Prosecute Non-Stranger Sexual Assault," *Voice*, 2009, Vol. 3.1, p. 3.

[182] Emma Sulkowicz, "A Call to Carry that Weight Together," *Columbia Spectator*, October 26, 2014, http://columbiaspectator.com/opinion/2014/10/26/call-carry-weight-together.

[183] Cathy Young, "Columbia Student: I Didn't Rape Her," *Daily Beast*, February 3, 2015, http://www.thedailybeast.com/articles/2015/02/03/columbia-student-i-didn-t-rape-her.html.

[184] Anonymous, "Why I Believe Emma Sulkowicz," *Columbia Spectator*, February 9, 2015, http://columbiaspectator.com/opinion/2015/02/09/why-i-believe-emma-sulkowicz.

[185] Jessica Luther, "Fighting Sexual Assault," *Austin Chronicle*, May 16, 2014, http://www.austinchronicle.com/news/2014-05-16/fighting-sexual-assault/.

[186] Tanya Somanader, "President Obama Launches the 'It's On Us' Campaign to End Sexual Assault on Campus," White House, September 19, 2014, https://www.whitehouse.gov/blog/2014/09/19/president-obama-launches-its-us-campaign-end-sexual-assault-campus.

[187] Michael Winerip, "Stepping Up to Stop Sexual Assault," *New York Times*, February 7, 2014, http://www.nytimes.com/2014/02/09/education/edlife/stepping-up-to-stop-sexual-assault.html.

[188] Lauren Chief Elk and Shaadi Devereaux, "The Failure of Bystander Intervention," *New Inquiry*, December 23, 2014, http://thenewinquiry.com/essays/failure-of-bystander-intervention/.

[189] Part of this section appeared in an earlier form in Jessica Luther, "How Football Culture Can Change Rape Culture," *Nation*, April 16, 2014, http://www.thenation.com/article/how-football-culture-can-change-rape-culture/.

[190] Tom Farrey and Nicole Noren, "Mizzou Did Not Pursue Alleged Assault," ESPN, January 24, 2014, http://espn.go.com/espn/otl/story/_/id/10323102/university-missouri-officials-did-not-pursue-rape-case-lines-investigation-finds.

[191] Chris Connelly, "Mizzou's Michael Sam Says He's Gay," ESPN, February 10, 2014, http://espn.go.com/espn/otl/story/_/id/10429030/michael-sam-missouri-tigers-says-gay.

[192] "Missouri's Campus Celebrates Michael Sam's Announcement," *Sports Illustrated*, February 10, 2014, http://www.si.com/college-football/2014/02/10/michael-sam-missouri-tigers-campus. Mike Florio, "Michael Sam Gets Standing Ovation at Missouri Basketball Game," *ProFootballTalk*, February 15, 2014, http://profootballtalk.nbcsports.com/2014/02/15/michael-sam-gets-standing-ovation-at-missouri-basketball-game/.

[193] Gwen Knapp, "Choosing His Loyalties," *Sports on Earth*, January 28, 2014, http://www.sportsonearth.com/article/67199852/former-missouri-football-player-rolandis-woodland-defends-sasha-menu-courey.

[194] http://www.umsystem.edu/ums/news/media_archives/02141401_news.

[195] Alan Scher Zagier, "Review: Mizzou Didn't Follow Federal Assault

Rules," Associated Press, April 11, 2014, http://collegefootball.ap.org/article/review-mizzou-didnt-follow-federal-assault-rules.

[196] Caroline Bauman, "Sasha Menu Courey Follow-Up: Reporting Sexual Assault Not Required for MU Faculty," *Missourian*, August 27, 2014, http://www.columbiamissourian.com/news/sasha-menu-courey-follow-up-reporting-sexual-assault-not-required/article_b649dcdd-ff57-5ed5-b8cc-d09f5221808a.html.

[197] "Man Up: Regina Rams Athlete Tackling Violence, Sexual Assault," CBC News, October 26, 2015, http://www.cbc.ca/news/canada/saskatchewan/university-of-regina-man-up-program-1.3289805.

[198] Adriana Christianson, "New U of R Campaigns Aim to Change Attitudes About Sexual Assault," *CJME*, October 26, 2015, http://cjme.com/article/266129/new-u-r-campaigns-aim-change-attitudes-about-sexual-assault.

[199] Tom Van Haaren, "Baker's Stand Against Abuse," ESPN, September 25, 2014, http://espn.go.com/college-sports/recruiting/football/story/_/id/11577936/football-recruit-jerome-baker-doing-part-stop-domestic-violence.

[200] Sarah Kogod, "Ohio State LB Jerome Baker Wants to Change How Athletes Talk About Sexual Violence," *SB Nation*, September 17, 2015, http://www.sbnation.com/2015/9/17/9105829/ohio-state-jerome-baker-is-changing-athletes-sexual-assault-2015.

[201] Ben Axelrod, "Meet Urban Meyer's Secret Weapon," *Bleacher Report*, August 25, 2015, http://bleacherreport.com/articles/2549161-meet-urban-meyers-yoda.

[202] Dan Zinski, "Texas Longhorns Dismiss Kendall Sanders, Montrel Meander," *Fansided*, August 3, 2014, http://fansided.com/2014/08/03/texas-longhorns-dismiss-kendall-sanders-montrel-meander/.

[203] https://www.youtube.com/watch?v=sFJtwqExF9k.

[204] Jessica Glenza, "Jameis Winston Suspended for Whole Game As FSU Extends Quarterback's Ban," *Guardian*, September 20, 2014, http://www.theguardian.com/sport/2014/sep/20/jameis-winston-fsu-ban-comments-football.

[205] http://videos.al.com/al/2014/10/jimbo_fisher_faces_the_media.html.

[206] Solomon Crenshaw Jr., "After Initially Refusing to Discuss Jameis Winston, Jimbo Fisher Says He's Willing to Discipline QB 'If The Facts Change,'" AL.com, October 20, 2014, http://www.al.com/sports/index.ssf/2014/10/hear_jimbo_fisher_address_ques.html.

[207] Bud Elliott, "Who Is Speaking to Florida State About Off-Field Issues and Student Athlete Life?" *SB Nation*, August 14, 2015, http://www.tomahawknation.com/2015/8/14/9153855/florida-state-behavior-trouble-fsu-off-field-speaker.

[208] Joe Douglass, "UO Hired Sex Offender to Talk Sexual Assault Awareness to Athletes," KVAL, September 28, 2014, http://kval.com/news/local/uo-hired-sex-offender-to-talk-sexual-assault-awareness-to-athletes-11-11-2015.

[209] Lauren Urban, "Bad Decision or Bad Character?" Ionian, October 25, 2011, http://www.ioniannews.com/opinion/columnists/article_97a58bf1-b51b-5b35-9811-75bf69a94c3f.html.

[210] Parts of this section appeared in an earlier form in Jessica Luther, "Can Coaches Be Trusted to End Hazing?" Vice Sports, October 27, 2014, https://sports.vice.com/en_us/article/can-coaches-be-trusted-to-end-hazing.

[211] Jessica Luther, "'We Felt Like We Were Above the Law': How the NCAA Endangers Women," Atlantic, September 26, 2013, http://www.theatlantic.com/entertainment/archive/2013/09/we-felt-like-we-were-above-the-law-how-the-ncaa-endangers-women/280004/.

[212] Terry Frei, "Jack Graham Fired as CSU Athletic Director, Calls Decision 'Surprising,' 'Disappointing,'" Denver Post, August 8, 2014, http://www.denverpost.com/colleges/ci_26302027/jack-graham-fired-csu-athletic-director. Jerry Carino and Keith Sergeant, "Rutgers AD Tim Pernetti Out After Mike Rice Firing," USA Today, April 5, 2013, http://www.usatoday.com/story/sports/ncaab/2013/04/05/ad-tim-pernetti-out-at-rutgers-after-mike-rice-firing/2056119/. Fritz Neighbor, "University of Montana Fires Football Coach, Athletic Director," Missourian, March 29, 2012, http://missoulian.com/news/local/university-of-montana-fires-football-coach-athletic-director/article_b7877268-79c0-11e1-92b3-0019bb2963f4.html. Nolan Clay and Robby Trammell, "TU Athletic Director Fired," News OK, December 4, 2012, http://newsok.com/article/3734705. Mark Schlabach, "Source: Georgia AD Evans Ousted," ESPN, July 4, 2010, http://espn.go.com/college-sports/news/story?id=5354373. "Kansas Athletic Director Al Bohl Fired," WTOL, April 9, 2003, http://www.wtol.com/story/1225086/kansas-athletic-director-al-bohl-fired.

[213] Part of this section appeared in an earlier form in Jessica Luther, "'We Felt Like We Were Above the Law': How the NCAA Endangers Women," Atlantic, September 26, 2013, http://www.theatlantic.com/entertainment/archive/2013/09/we-felt-like-we-were-above-the-law-how-the-ncaa-endangers-women/280004/.

[214] Peter Berkes, "Hey College Coaches, Stop Recruiting with Creepy Female Celebrity Photoshops," SB Nation, April 24, 2015, http://www.sbnation.com/college-football/2015/4/24/8489991/college-coaches-recruiting-creepy-photoshops.

[215] Tim Polzer, "Mark Emmert: NCAA Won't Budge on Paying College

Athletes," *Sports Illustrated*, September 17, 2013, http://www.si.com/si-wire/2013/09/17/mark-emmert-ncaa-paying-athletes. Sara Ganim, "Paying College Athletes Would Hurt Traditions, NCAA Chief Emmert Testifies," CNN, June 19, 2014, http://www.cnn.com/2014/06/19/us/ncaa-obannon-lawsuit-trial/.

[216] Jessica Luther, "'We Felt Like We Were Above the Law': How the NCAA Endangers Women," *Atlantic*, September 26, 2013, http://www.theatlantic.com/entertainment/archive/2013/09/we-felt-like-we-were-above-the-law-how-the-ncaa-endangers-women/280004/.

[217] This section largely from Jessica Luther, "Changing the Narrative," *Sports on Earth*, May 7, 2014, http://www.sportsonearth.com/article/74027694/sports-media-needs-a-better-understanding-of-how-to-report-on-sexual-assault-cases.

[218] Dave Zirin, "The NCAA Should Shut Down Notre Dame's Football Program," *Nation*, November 29, 2010, http://www.thenation.com/article/ncaa-should-shut-down-notre-dames-football-program/.

[219] Julie DiCaro, "Why I Believe Jameis Winston's Accuser," *Deadspin*, December 9, 2013, http://deadspin.com/why-i-believe-jameis-winstons-accuser-1479782169.

[220] Melissa McEwan, "Rape Culture 101," *Shakesville*, October 9, 2009, http://www.shakesville.com/2009/10/rape-culture-101.html.

[221] David Leonard, "Kasandra Michelle Perkins: We Must Say Her Name," *Feminist Wire*, December 3, 2012, http://www.thefeminist-wire.com/2012/12/kasandra-michelle-perkins/.

[222] Josh Katzowitz, "Why #FSUTwitter Is Football's Most-Feared Digital Mob," *Kernel*, August 30, 2015, http://kernelmag.dailydot.com/issue-sections/headline-story/14148/fsu-twitter-mob-jameis-winston/.

[223] http://www.ncaa.org/health-and-safety/sports-fandom-and-ncaa-student-athlete.

[224] Eric Simons, "The Psychology of Why Sports Fans See Their Teams As Extensions of Themselves," *Washington Post*, January 30, 2015, https://www.washingtonpost.com/opinions/the-psychology-of-why-sports-fans-see-their-teams-as-extensions-of-themselves/2015/01/30/521e0464-a816-11e4-a06b-9df2002b86a0_story.html.

[225] Richard Lapchick, "The 2012 Associated Press Sports Editors Racial and Gender Report Card," the Institute for Diversity and Ethics in Sport, March 1, 2013.

[226] "The State of Women in the US Media, 2014," Women's Media Center, p. 5.

[227] Part of this section appeared in an earlier form in Jessica Luther, "Who We Talk About When Athletes Are Accused of Sexual Assault," *Vice Sports*, October 14, 2014, https://sports.vice.com/en_

us/article/who-we-talk-about-when-athletes-are-accused-of-sexual-assault.

[228] Jessica Luther, "The NFL's Domestic Violence Problem and Our Race Problem," *Vice Sports*, September 25, 2014, https://sports.vice.com/en_us/article/the-nfls-domestic-violence-problem-and-our-race-problem.

Conclusion

[229] Dan Solomon and Jessica Luther, "Silence at Baylor," *Texas Monthly*, August 20, 2015, http://www.texasmonthly.com/article/silence-at-baylor/.